OFF WATCH
WITH
OLD HARRY

By the same author:

Cruising: A Manual for Small Cruiser Sailing
Up the Creek with Old Harry
Old Harry's Dog Watch
Anchor's Aweigh

OFF WATCH
WITH
OLD HARRY

The funny side of sailing

Des Sleightholme

ADLARD COLES NAUTICAL
London

This edition published 1997 by Adlard Coles Nautical
an imprint of A & C Black (Publishers) Ltd
35 Bedford Row, London WC1R 4JH

First published by Adlard Coles 1989
Reprinted by Adlard Coles Nautical 1997

ISBN 0-7136-4828-7

A CIP catalogue record for this book is available from
the British Library.

Printed and bound in Great Britain by
The Cromwell Press, Melksham, Wiltshire

Contents

Most of the following pieces are reprinted with the kind permission of *Yachting Monthly*.

Preface

The collection of bits and pieces in this book has much in common with the ship's 'shakings bag', which contained an assortment of odds and ends of rope, cord and canvas likely to come in handy for the mariner in search of a bit of lashing. More important though was that it discouraged him from hacking off a piece from a coil of good stuff – a crime comparable to a boarding house guest wantonly helping himself to a new toilet roll when there still remains a fathom of heavy duty tissue and a cardboard tube in the loo. I hope that somewhere in this shakings bag the reader may find a short end that suits the mood.

Old Harry – fact and fiction

At intervals during the past thirty years an individual called Old Harry has cropped up on my typewriter, a militant traditionalist and improviser of maniacal ingenuity who has blundered in and out of my writing as the fancy took him. On an Old Harry day the old swine would take over my first waking thoughts, haunt me from bathroom to breakfast table then accompany me on a three-mile walk to the office. The route being straight, without distractions, I would amble along, notebook in hand, muttering, grunting and occasionally scribbling. Mothers would gather their young ones close, dogs raising a leg in salute would eye me and lower it in uncertainty and passing police car drivers would slow down and finger chins speculatively. Such was an Old Harry day.

He was a real person – two people really. There was the turkey-necked Alec, built like an ironing board, who on Sunday mornings would stand with his backside to the fire, wearing a long nightshirt and his peaked cap, and play the accordion. His wife was Chairwoman of the local writers' circle, sang basso profundo in the choir and dedicated the rest of the time to sorting out Alec – a task as formidable as trying to straighten up the leaning tower of Pisa. His other half was 'Snappy', an Essex longshoreman whose wife had left him, "er up the line' he called her. Snappy was short-legged, squat and had the sort of face you see in cave drawings. He was at constant war with local authority. He ran a shilling sicker-boat off the Southend beach which he packed with trippers far in excess of the regulation maximum of twelve. 'You can hear them a' pleasurin' of themselves, a' carryin' on like seagulls 'ammerin' sprats,' he would exclaim. Packed in chest to back there lacked only the manacles and groans of a slaver.

Both men dealt in the restoration and sale of decrepit boats to unsuspecting nincompoop novices, both were totally without conscience. Alec pioneered ferro-cement, a material of great potential for the repair of craft so advanced in decay that nails would no longer hold. It was said that one such renovation (which owed more to hod and trowel than to saw and adze) was sailed away by her delighted jug-eared new owners and hit Ryde Pier; a cloud of cement dust hung over the town for days and there were beautiful sunsets for the next month.

He used to buy old barges, then break them up for firewood, spending a whole winter chopping them down into threepenny bundles. I once agreed to steer one such ancient vessel while he towed her from Cowes to his base. The barge couldn't sink completely, being built of timber, but with decks awash, swept by small waves at intervals, I was forced to leap into the air as they passed, a sight which seen from the shore by a religiously minded old gentleman of poor vision had a profound effect on his faith.

Snappy sold boats by strength of personality and barefaced lies. 'Why, I've rowed that boat across a dewey lawn, mate.' Summoned to the Town Hall to account for his sicker-boat crimes and faced by a panel of Foreshore Committee elders across a table he seized the front edge and tipped it and them over backwards in a tangle of sock suspender and art silk bloomer. In retribution they let loose upon him a Board of Trade Inspector to check his boat. 'Now look,' said this official, 'this fire extinguisher is empty! I shall be back next week and I will expect to find it filled and in working order.'

During ordinary conversation Snappy had a habit of grasping the front of your jacket and rocking you to and fro by way of emphasis. He gripped me and gave a preliminary rock. 'So I puts it in me barrer and takes it up to me mate at the fire station, right?' he rocked. ''E fills it wiv foam an' I barrers it back, right?' I staggered and nodded hastily. 'Back comes this hinspector and what does 'e do? Wot 'e does, mate, is FIRE IT ORF, that's wot 'e done, SET IT A'GOIN'.' I stared down into a scarlet face racked with intolerable grief. He rocked me into the gutter. 'All me lovely new foam, mate, flyin' everywhere, an' there I am a' trying' ter catch it in me cap!' And thus Old Harry.

J.D. Sleightholme

*'A good mug o' tea,' Snappy said to me once, 'and a nice bit o'
fat pork sets you up, mate. Why, you can feel it on yer chest a'
lyin' there, a' nurishin' of yer all night long.' Well, I'm none too
sure about the fat pork. Lying in my bunk on a North Sea Race
once I opened my eyes just as the farmer-mate opened the
pressure cooker and, fishing around in the steam, lifted out this
great juddering gobbet of 'nurishment'. I clapped hand to
mouth and rushed on deck. The tea, though, now that's another
matter.*

Trouble brewing

In the great era of moustache cups, modesty fronts and
the celluloid dicky every yacht carried a paid hand in the
fo'c's'le like some resident sage, tyrant and scourge of the
rich, and his head-shakings, eye-rolling and sucking of
teeth (phenomena exhibited at the first mention of going
to sea) dictated the movements of the vessel. You might
find a dozen yachts all sheltering from the same immi-
nent but fictitious gale. A cloud of steam like a working
model of Table Mountain would hang over the largest,
hovering above a well-battened forehatch beneath which
all hands had gathered for a brew and for frank and open
discussion of their various owners, their parsimony and
hilarious ineptitude as yachtsmen. Those were tea parties
such as the world will never see again, where cucumber
sandwich or garibaldi biscuit would win the twisted lip
of scorn. Those huge enamel mugs, deep-etched with the
patina of past brews and containing a permanent sugary
sump of 'nurishment' are gone beyond recall.

Nowadays we have a wealth of jolly crockery and a host
of instant beverages, each guaranteed to induce healthy
sleep like a rap with a hand-spike, plus unbounded en-

1

ergy, promotion to departmental boss and a Tesco-Georgian front door. Yet tea of a sort remains the traditional drink for British watchkeepers and which has made us what we are today and shrunk the Royal Navy like boiling a wool sweater.

The watchkeeper off duty, deep in nightmare-infested coma, can only be aroused by having a mug of scalding tea rammed under his gobbling chops with the cry of 'You're on, mate', a humane and sensitive custom which has a dynamic effect. The lucky recipient, who has spent the past three hours bicycling in his sleeping bag like last man in the Tour de France, jerks upright sobbing for his mother. 'No hurry,' soothes his benefactor, 'It's Force six on the nose and slashing down. You've got three minutes.'

Foreigners move in constant dread of British hospitality. 'Come aboard, my wife is just going to put the kettle on,' hails the generous owner, enunciating with care and implying some bizarre fashion show. They confer hissingly and rapidly behind their sprayhood, hands are spread and eyes are rolled but accept they must. They will be plied endlessly with fig biscuits and Earl Grey, addressed at dictation speed, despite a fluent command of English, and lectured on the superiority of the English sausage.

Old Harry regards the pouring of English tea down foreign gullets as a beneficial necessity like the dipping of sheep and the pursuit of woolly aphids. 'Why, dog-bite-me, they ain't acquired the taste on account they don't know the secret, d'you see,' he explains. With a frowning attention to detail that would make the Japanese Tea Ceremony seem like a cardboard cupful on the 5.30 out of Euston, he sets about remedying this educational defect and thereby treating his guests to a glimpse of a statelier way of life.

Whipping his shaving stick out of the spare mug and buffing it on his sleeve he blows down the spout of the teapot with all the delicacy of a lady flautist, shovels in tea with a generosity that wins gasps of gratitude, adds the molasses and, with an air of consecration, pours on

2

the boiling water. There is no effete choice here of a slice of lemon or a twist of mint in lieu of milk. Removing matchstick spigots from the tin of condensed, and applying pursed lips to one hole, he projects a glutinous and generous jet into each mug. With spoons stuck upright like port-hand beacons he hands a mug to each eager guest, raises his own and imbibes deeply. 'Real English tea,' he identifies in booming stereophonic tones from its depths. 'Get it acrost you.' Petrified, they take tentative sips then jerk upright with rolling eye, clutching their throats and stampeding shorewards. On a quiet night Old Harry can be heard supping his tea from half a parish away, the mellow slurp followed by the 'Ahhh' of appreciation, like Watts' beam engine passing top dead centre. With head thrown back and teaspoon drumming furrowed brow, he

reaches for the nectar of the dregs like some monstrous Amazonian insect busy with giant orchid.

The effects of tea on the prosecution of the navigator's ancient art is not properly understood. Mother down below sticks her head out with the caution of the canny and surveys sea and sky. She notes an absence of rocks, shipping, whales, waterspouts, tidal waves and hurricanes and deems it a suitable time to brew up. The ship is bobbing along on a broad reach under Autohelm, there is forty miles to go on the same heading and father is busy with his plastic sextant – a sure sign that he has absolutely nothing else to do. Within the time it takes to slosh water over teabags, add milk and sugar and send up this delicious infusion in the washing-up basin a strange metamorphosis has taken place. Father adopts a crouching attitude and begins peering around urgently. 'Not now, not now. Can't you see I'm navigating?' he cries brokenly, bobbing up and down like a parrot on a perch. In offshore racing circles this tea ritual is more elaborate and spiced with the heavy thespian touch of the shuddering sigh and the eye upraised to an all-seeing but uncompetitive deity. 'And DON'T give the helmsman a biscuit,' the owner pleads, as if so rich a diet might prove fatal.

Tea and its vital place aboard the British yacht is demonstrated with force by the ocean voyaging singlehanders, dividing their time between rigging jury rudders, trying to photograph themselves taking a sun sight and searching for their souls like lost season tickets. They may also have to brew up unusual quantities of tea in order to placate their sponsors, a duty revealed on their tape recorders at a later date. '2145 GMT just hit a sleeping whale,' it states in shaken tones, 'need a cup of Simpsons Golden Blend.' The recorder gives vent to a series of clangs and scratchings. '0020 enjoying cup of Simpson's family Quik Brew, whale still following astern.' There follows a resounding crash, a tinkle and a gulp.

The British traveller abroad armed with Doctor Collis-Browne's powerful nostrum to ward off every evil and ill from Attaturk's Revenge to werewolves, demands morning tea with the unwavering fixity of purpose of Jason after his Golden Fleece. Although the laughable infusion brought to his bedside is a wretched substitute, it provides a faint reminder of the white cliffs of Dover and the double yellow lines of home. In my own case it takes a full pint of bog-brown syrup to get my steam up in the morning. After the first gulp it is like watching Frankenstein's monster react to the flash of lightning: a deep shudder runs through me, my spine straightens out like a fireman's hose under pressure and my soul comes zipping back off the astral plane as if I'd caught my braces over the bedpost.

Prior to the discovery that started me on a writing career – that women's magazines paid a guinea a time for readers' letters published (I dreamed up some right little sizzlers) – there was a period when I dabbled in winkle picking, lobstering, yacht delivery and skippering as a means of livelihood. I drove a speedboat towing models for a mad inventor and after I sank it I became master of this horrid little motor cruiser, before it sank.

Keep calm

When you opened the throttles there was no chesty bellow of power, no belligerent crackling roar; her twin Handy Billies just popped away like boiling porridge. Her deck saloon-cum-wheelhouse was the sort of glass erection found on seaside esplanades where bed-and-breakfast holidaymakers eat egg sandwiches and watch the rain; she had her steering compass offset to increase the fun of navigation and her wheel should have had a presentation barometer set in the middle. She slept two right aft in comfort, two right forward in defiance of the laws of gravity. But, she was my command as charter skipper for one month. Until I sank her.

The first charter was a walkover. All the party wanted was day outings from Portsmouth and they knew less about boats than Ivan the Terrible knew about Mothercare. There was a dishy little children's nanny who wore a floaty summer dress and blue panties, who took to standing on the foredeck, slap in my delighted line of vision as I stood at the wheel (until 'madam' noted my preoccupation and called her the hell back inside). The rest of the party took up window seats around the deckhouse like a coach tour. The only sour note was Mister Patrick.

We had him with us for a day. At some time he must have read *The Yachtsman's Weekend Book*. He wore the lot; reefer, cheese-cutter, pale pants and socks with clocks. He had rocking-horse teeth and his mission was to prove me incompetent. As a child I had been baffled by educational toys and so his day was pleasant and rewarding. We backed out from the pontoon and I narrowly missed a ferry; we went ahead and with nanny on the foredeck I was all set to hit another until I heard him making a whinnying sound. Then he began yipping about a morse signal that was being sent from the control tower. 'Signals man, SIGNALS,' he fretted. I stared uncomprehendingly at the stuttering morse. 'Yacht . . . Daisybell . . . free . . . to proceed,' I invented, swerving around a car ferry. An aircraft carrier was filling the entrance. We squeezed past, gazing up the nostrils of the ranked matelots and escaped to open water.

We squared away for Cowes while nanny made tea. Mister Patrick had the charts out, navigating like Magellan in a dust storm while I steered and munched Marie biscuits. 'You have Ryde West Middle coming abeam NOW,' he roared suddenly in my ear. I puffed crumbs in his direction gratefully. He was everywhere at once, bounding from window to window like a bird in a cage, back again to note compass heading (singularly unrewarding considering its siting) and then bounding off again to chart or binoculars. It was half flood, so I cut across the Shrape. He had *Reed's* and the pilot book out. 'On no account go near the Shrape,' he cautioned, searching around for it. I assured him I would avoid it like bubonic and headed for the breakwater.

Now that cruiser was no more than twenty-five miserable feet long and she drew less than a redshank with its legs down. Suddenly he cottoned to the truth that we were *out of the channel*. 'STOP ENGINES,' he screamed. I took the porridge off the boil. 'Great Scott man, you're out of the channel,' he sobbed. Then he shamed me.

I had a lot of mates in Cowes. He made me take *Daisybell* right out round the Consort and then he sounded us in, mid-channel, all the way, on the handlead! I steered with my head down, collar turned up while he sounded in a great ringing baritone, 'By the Mark Seven' and all the rest of it. We got Mark Five off the pontoon, and-a-half-four and deep four and a raspberry from the dockies waiting on the floating bridge. On the way back to Portsmouth he dipped to a Royal Naval frigate and then stepped ashore into some dog-dirt. That was the first charter.

The second and fateful charter was in Chichester Harbour and my charterer was a retired naval Commander with his wife and kids. The aim was to day-cruise, spend-

ing the occasional night on board. Nothing exacting or exciting and nothing remotely bearing upon risk or discomfort. The weather was settled and perfect, hot and windless, so what could possibly go wrong? If I had studied the portents, read the sheep's entrails or even considered Sod's Law I might have realised that these are the worst of conditions for things going wrong.

It was the top of the spring tides – big ones. We popped our way down harbour and turned to starboard into the Thorney Channel, passing between the big marker beacons at the entrance over a shimmer of still, glassy water that danced in the heat haze. Our dinghy astern rode an oiled silk wake that fanned out to hiss softly among the grasses as we passed. Off West Thorney we anchored for tea.

We sat on deck. The tide brimmed higher and higher until the saltings were hidden and the big fat muddy bubbles rode by and the whole wide marshscape lay full and tranquil around us. We poured another cup all round and ate Lyon's Jam Roll.

I was about to learn a valuable lesson. I was to learn that there is never, ever, more than one skipper in any one boat and that he is responsible and in charge. One skipper, one can, and he carries it.

I suppose it must have been me who offered to wash up while the Commander took her out of the channel. I must have reasoned that Commanders are Commanders and that all are at home on the bridge and the fact that there are Commanders who command a Paymaster's desk never occurred to me. The way out was plainly marked – even if the beacons were by then almost submerged. The chart showed the channel and a row of submerged piles across the saltings – even if the whole lot was now one vast glittering expanse of water.

I was blowing down the spout of the teapot when it happened. We were popping along smoothly when suddenly I found myself on my back. There was a deafening wooden bang – up went the bows – then down in a grinding shuddering lurch as the stern came up. Then we were level again.

I bounded on deck, clutching the pot. The Commander and I gazed at each other, mouths opening and closing, then we both began yelling at once. Dead astern there showed, briefly, the raw yellow pine of a propeller-chewed stump. I shot below to sound the well. I was saved that trouble; up from beneath the saloon carpet came a gurgling stream of oily water. There was a belt-driven bilge pump on the engine; I slammed it into gear. Almost simultaneously the twin flywheels sent up twin sprays of foulness that lubricated the belt and the pump stopped. Hand pump! I had stripped it down only the week before but though I wagged the handle with the speed of light the carpet still floated. Buckets! The Commander's wife and I were soon splashing around down there like a pantomime whitewash act, but still the water rose.

On deck the Commander, still at the wheel, was yelling. 'We must all KEEP CALM,' he screamed, rolling his eyes at our slithering activities. 'Dora, get aft . . . *pack the bag.*' There was no panic. We all came over dead British. I was tempted to dress for dinner. Dora went aft at controlled speed and began hurling clothes into a suitcase and I went up for a quick look around. Both engines were flat out, porridge boiling like Mount Etna. The initial rush of water, always more dramatic during the first minutes while the narrow confines of the bilges are filling, had not yet reached the electrics. The Commander had his jaw set; his knuckles were white with gripping that absurd barometer steering wheel. The flag shall not fall boys, our finest moment was still to come.

If there is a Guinness Book of Records entry for packing suitcases, then Dora had it staked down. Up she came from below, lugging it, while the kids watched, pop-eyed with excitement. 'The dinghy, the dinghy, get it into the dinghy, woman,' the Commander commanded. I was due back at the pumps but I watched, fascinated. Now you know and I know what happens when you pull in a dinghy that's towing astern; you need both hands. Which means that you have to put down your suitcase. And you know and I also know, with the weight of bitter experience, when you let go of the painter in order to pick up the suitcase, in order to chuck it into the dinghy . . . It went bobbing astern, the lid was ajar as if champing on a pyjama leg like some strange sea monster tackling an unsatisfactory snack. It wallowed, burped air and sank. A short time later so did we.

The surprise visit by some obscure relative, not seen in thirty years and, following the visit, not likely to be seen for another thirty, is an event common to most families. He wore sock suspenders, he really did. He was the complete antithesis of all I hold dear, a whimp of the first order. Against my background of boats and people with antifouling paint on the peaks of their caps Percy stuck out like a Portacabin in an area of natural beauty. So I took him sailing.

A day out with Percy

'Having Percy down' (a turn of phrase smacking of a rugby tackle and a sly jab with an elbow) begins innocently enough with a simple invitation. You haven't seen each other in years. Ritual preliminaries must first be dispensed with; who is in which hospital with what, who carries which firm *literally* on his two shoulders and how Margaret's girl outgrew her strength, failed her Os and caused the milkman to walk into his own tailboard. Then you go aboard.

Metamorphosis. From the moment you begin trundling the dinghy down the hard Percy goes into his act. 'Here, let me help,' he calls, flinging his full weight on the trolley towbar. The stern rockets into the air. Your regular mate, Ned (retired, forty years in surgical knitwear) goes soaring upwards like a flighting lark. 'WHEEEP!' he hollers in falsetto agony, clutching. 'Oh sorry!' apologises Percy, wrenching the towbar upwards. The dinghy transom slams down, pinning Ned's toes to the concrete. 'PHAAAW!' gasps Ned.

Alert now to this man's awful potential you seat him in the dinghy with the elaborate care of a museum curator packing amphorae. He sits clutching the gun'le right aft. Ned boards, watching him narrowly, and you follow, sitting daintily beside Percy. You push off. Now then, *in normal circumstances* this is a pleasant row in some of the most picturesque waters in the country, a scene rich in history and wildlife. Someone-or-other once painted it. It was mentioned in Domesday, guardedly. Ned takes four full strokes. 'Why,' proclaims Percy, 'you can actually see the bottom.' He lunges sideways and hangs his great wobbling wattles overboard. The boat lurches, Ned misses

a full stroke. We note that he is wearing grip-toe socks. 'WHAAAAF!' he observes, hurtling backwards.

Getting under way – a busy and animated picture, for the ebb is well away lads, and the open sea calls. Percy plays the role of middle skittle, skipping nimbly back and forth, unerringly placing himself dead in line with whomsoever is going where. To localise him, so to speak, you give him the topping lift to hold. 'Lower an inch when I say *now*,' you explain, articulating with great care. 'When you say *now*?' he asks, making quite certain. 'That's right, when I say *now*,' you confirm. The boom end hammers down driving your cap over your ears like a pickle jar lid. Up forward Ned has had the forehatch closed on his fingers and he is making a curiously whinnying, humming sound like a transformer station under peak load.

What can you give Percy to do that will keep him right the hell out of your way? Answer: you can give him the mooring buoy to hold, finally letting it go upon hearing the clearly delivered command to do so. He holds it, feet braced, frowning slightly. You explain in a quiet, friendly, albeit tremulous, voice; 'I – shall – say DROP THE MOORING.' There is a frantic swipe with the boathook and a dash to start the engine while Ned fends off the two-tone Noah's Ark astern. He gropes for and finds the tiller under the cockpit cover, voice boomingly begging for directions in his tented little prison. He stands on a packed lunch. Egg and cress.

The run downriver is uneventful. Percy manages to unreeve the spinaker halyard in the belief that he was hauling up the jib. He stands on the gimballed cooker while making coffee for all with gravy browning. We remove the dry powder fire extinguisher and hide it wrapped in an old coat. He has been awaiting his moment and it finally arrives. We are on a dead run. Two huge freighters and a pilot launch are barrelling upriver with little room to clear. It is a tense moment. A monumental gybe is pending and the mainsheet is foul of Percy's shoulder bag. He sticks his great mottled chops up through the hatch. 'Could you show me how to work the toilet please?' he asks very politely.

There is little more to tell. He was given the helm for a short while on the way back, but we discovered that walking with your toes curled up limits mobility and the intakes of breath, cringing, wincing, ducking and clenching of teeth inhibits conversation. I was in the hatch keeping a low profile and Ned was on deck forward. 'Percy,' I said tactfully, 'perhaps you'd better give Ned the helm now.' Percy then gave Ned the helm. He *took* it to him.

And so ashore again, healthily tired after a long day in God's fresh air, tanned by sun and wind. You row Percy ashore (Ned having opted for two trips).

'Well, thanks for a truly marvellous day,' laughs Percy. Firmly he presses his foot down on the gunwhale as he disembarks, holding it there with masterly skill and timing while water gurgles and the boat settles under you. He notes your curious situation in the water below him. 'Oh,' he says, 'Can I give you a hand?'

'Yes,' you say, 'Oh YES!'

A casual observer commenting later confessed that he had been puzzled to note that the two men had changed positions so rapidly.

In East Anglia your nearest foreign coasts are those of Holland and Belgium, separated by seventy-odd miles of North Sea, as nasty a stretch of water as you'd find, strewn with sandbanks like cow-pats in a meadow and ploughed by hurtling freighters. The seas are short, steep and vindictive and sailing them is like bicycling over a celery bed. It is plagued by hazy visibility and fast but unpredictable tidal streams. There is little rest on such passages and any skipper who goes below for a caulk does so on the call-me-for-any-reason-or-none-at-all basis. He may even have sunk into his first coma when the call comes. 'Would you like to come up and look at this?' somebody invites, as if showing off his holiday snaps. Father is out of the roost with ballistic speed and on the tiller in a flying tackle as forty thousand tons goes drumming past a biscuit's toss away; a hell of a big biscuit. He hangs there counting portholes.

After a passage like that he has a psychopathic desire to berth the boat, enmesh her with ropes and curl up in a foetal ball like an anchovy. The visitors' berths are full of fathers, recovering.

A long wick-end

The agricultural desolation of flattened hedgerow and drained marshland which greets the ruffled and panting spring migrant is no more daunting than the *visiteur*'s berth awaiting the exhausted yachtsman at the conclusion of his passage. It can vary between a sort of nautical purdah stuck out on the end of the most distant pontoon and reeking stretch of wall next to the fish dock where the first yacht alongside, like some unwitting queen bee, is soon to be buried under a buzzing horde of later arrivals.

'We're in luck,' laughs father without quite realising what sort of luck. 'Right next to the ladder. Why, I think we might well stay for a couple of days.' In fact it is nearer

16

a week before they escape from the day-long thudding procession across their deck of strangers carrying sponge bag and towel.

The rafting up ritual continues with boat after boat, until the outside one is swaying precariously half-way across the harbour like top man on a human pyramid – a nasty shock for your novice still powdered with blackboard chalk from his evening classes and sternly briefed in the *mores* of mooring.

To get ashore he has to face a rocking obstacle course of guardrails, legging it over each with the painful slowness of a penitent during Holy Week. He learns that there is a rigid social rule compelling him to keep his gaze averted from cockpit and window as if either might reveal some scene of scorching intimacy. Rails are climbed as if they were electrified and the route lies forward of each mast but skirting open hatches and their titillating secrets.

A mini-tonner with a mast like an orthopaedic walking stick rolls violently and a stubbled, hung-over face peers up resentfully, groans and subsides. The television screen forehatch of a low-budget lifeboat conversion offers the glimpse of a Channel Four playlet of adult candour and on the next boat a domestic ding-dong is working up to full throttle. 'Oh, thank you; thank you very much,' comes a female voice empty of gratitude. Pans clatter. 'All I said was . . .' follows a male rumble.

He clambers onwards; children erupt and dogs snarl. Finally comes a Westerly from Grimsby (radar reflector right side up and double clips on all hoses) where the owner follows him with dustpan and brush. Awaiting his arrival is the berthing master to check on the duration of his intended stay. 'You have a long wick-end?' the man challenges, disturbingly.

Then there is the matter of The Ladder. Oily iron rungs in the wall lead giddily skyward. At the top and descending is a Brit with a shopping bag of croissants held in his teeth. He is wearing 1940-style shorts which offer to those waiting below a prospect not unlike a bell-ringer's view of the belfry lacking only the house-martin's nest. 'Sorry to hold you up,' he mumbles indistinctly. 'I'm sure you can see my little dilemma.'

There is a shade less privacy in the visitor's (*visiteur*'s) berth than one might hope to find under a cucumber frame. Day-long, children patrol in it their quest for further education and each porthole becomes a raree show, each

hatch as rich with hurrying animation as an overturned stone on the seashore. There is father, a dedicated bowel man, who has waited until all his crew are ashore before beginning his contemplative vigil up forward watched by unblinking seven-year-olds.

On another boat there is the moving spectacle of a retired Colonel of Horse Guards struggling to get both feet into one leg of his trousers, simultaneously closing the forehatch on his own head. There is a resonant thud as he succeeds and sinks slowly from view.

Nobody can hope to enjoy the outside berth for very long. The arrival and departure of boats throughout the day shuffles them to the centre of the pack in a sort of nautical high-cockalorum. There is the morning mass exodus of crews with pink and smiling faces, soon to meet the swell of the ocean's broad bosom and take on the hue of ancient documents, and there is the evening influx, haggard passagemakers still wearing their tomato soup moustaches and standing on a cockpit compost of biscuit crumbs and apple cores. They grapple alongside with great determination.

Innocent children at play in the path of a road roller, the unsuspecting community watches the approach of Old Harry but, as his battered cranse iron inclines towards them, a ripple of unease runs through the watchers as at the lighting of some beacon fire on the windy downs. Ordinarily the side-splitting antics of manoeuvring newcomers are noted with the pitiless relish of vultures eyeing the staggering approach of a buffalo to the dried-up waterhole, but smiles snap off as his bowsprit, Kitchener's pointing finger, levels and steadies on the two-tone power cruiser in the outer berth.

What follows next is pure Greek drama. The owner, recommending his soul to his Maker like some supermarket check-out offer, commits the sorry error of trying to sit up suddenly on his sun lounger just as the bowsprit commences its exploratory sweep of the afterdeck. Fifteen feet of varnished pitchpine capped by an economy size jar of Nivea is an unsettling sight. A big blonde on all fours wearing a bikini with a high-risk frontage scuttles ahead of it like a runaway sweet trolley.

Later, as Old Harry makes his way ashore loaded with empty fuel drums, his booming trunnel-booted progress flushes out those still below decks like a sulphur candle down a rat-hole. He reaches a diminutive French cruiser where the stacked sailbags on the foredeck force a diversion via the cockpit in which a picnic is in progress consisting largely of wine bottles and iron ramrods of bread. A muscular lady, wearing a sun-top like a cargo sling designed by Brunel, is slicing bits off what appears to be a mummified grey ferret. Old Harry sweeps off his cap revealing a bleached scalp rarely glimpsed outside Magistrate's Court. *'Par donny me monsewer, madam,'* he says, lapsing fluently into the language as he tiptoes with crunching inaccuracy through the scattered feast, *'avec voo bon happytits.'*

As if his arrival was not traumatic enough, his departure is to demonstrate depths of seamanship hitherto unplumbed. Having by then gravitated to the middle of the little colony his going is to blast the dawn serenity like the SAS kicking a door down. At four o'clock next morning, with some forty unsuspecting people asleep, shadowy figures begin creeping from boat to boat, passing lines outside-all and all inside-outside while Old Harry, orchestrator of the impending bedlam, stands crotch deep in a mounting tangle of dripping coir watching with approval. He starts the engine.

The crackling blast of din prompts every dog within a three-mile radius into howling protest and the echoes come blasting back from hillside and wall. Like pop-up toasters, forty sleepers jerk upright in their bunks and forty sickening thuds are followed by forty oaths in five languages. From hatch and companionway rear angry faces myopic with hangover, gums champing in the search for suitable words.

To extract a boat from the middle of a raft-up calls for an act of faith akin to that of Moses parting the Red Sea. The trick is to close the gap behind you before it can gape too wide and open out like a split carcass on the butcher's slab; a feat of dexterity comparable to wrenching open a hen-house door and grabbing one old boiler before the rest take wing.

It would call for two fingers more skilful than mine to pen an accurate picture of what follows but perhaps the sacking of Panama might be a close parallel. In the wan light of dawn figures attired variously in pyjama bottoms, tops or Y-fronts dance and yell amidst a frenzy of roaring engines and the threshing of dinghy paddles while hurling ropes, advice and genetic speculation on Old Harry's origins.

Aboard the Westerly from Grimsby (radar reflector right way up) the owner reads aloud in a strong voice from the *Admiralty Manual of Seamanship*, Part One.

*All my best years of sailing were under gaff rig and I have a
deep affection for it, with its deadeyes, gammon irons, fids,
saddles, travellers, rawhide, tallow and beeswax. Nowadays,
though, there is a bit of a cult feeling about gaff rig. The Mr
Birks of my imagination can be seen rocking around in their
vast thighboots and sweltering in authentic 'gansies' under a
hot July sun. It is not unlikely that the Stock Exchange floor
may on occasion show a line of muddy prints extending back to
Faversham Creek, and not a few executive briefcases, if opened
unexpectedly, would reveal a pair of galvanised rowlocks and a
ball of whipping twine. Knock the gaffers I may but I also have
a warm regard for them.*

Clean thoughts and cold gaffs

On my eighteenth birthday Dad took me for a country
walk and told me all about pollen. It wasn't very inter-
esting. I hadn't known where babies came from though
or that dad was a bumble-bee.

'There is something else you should know,' Dad said,
stopping dead in his tracks. I ran into him from behind and
bent my frisbee. 'Stop fiddling with your frisbee Norman
and listen carefully,' he went on. 'As a healthy young
person with normal healthy appetites there will be, huh,
certain temptations to which you will, huh, be exposed.'

'Yes Dad,' I replied twisting my woggle (for I was
in full scout uniform and covered with badges like a
mended air-bed).

'You must be told about – *gaffrig*,' Dad said through
clenched teeth.

'What's agffh igg?' I enquired. He ignored me.

'There's nothing, huh, unnatural about gaffrig, nothing
to, huh, snigger about in corners – and stop working your

clean-cut features so convulsively,' he chided gently, staring up into my clean-cut young features, for I am six foot one and built like a music stand. Once, on sports day and crouched in readiness for the 100 metre sprint, an old lady mistook me for a bamboo table and placed her Thermos and sponge fingers on my back. We strode along in silence for a while and my clean young mind was in turmoil. I had heard stories about gaff rig in the school lavs and Smith Minor once showed me a *picture*. I felt my open countenance burning. What with my scout hat and huge ears I looked like a defective pop-up toaster.

'I have made, huh, certain arrangements with a business colleague who owns one of these, huh, gaffers for you to have an experience,' Dad said. 'You are a pure-minded young windsurfer . . .' He paused, choked with emotion. 'Just be strong lad, strong for your mother's sake and mine.' He stopped abruptly, his chin wobbling.

To distract him I gave my pee-whit patrol call and demonstrated how this bird will feign a broken wing to lure predators away from the nest. 'Peee-WHIT,' I cried, running in circles flapping one arm. A man going by on a tractor, watching, drove through the side of a barn.

It was a blazing Friday afternoon in July when Dad's business colleague, Mr Birk of Birk & Wally (Pinner) Ltd, picked me up in his executive Rover and drove me down to Hopeless Creek where his authentic restored whelk prattler *Mud Harvester* was moored. He pulled the Rover off the road on to the grass verge. I thought that pushing would have been easier. There was a gent's convenience nearby. 'Wait here boy,' Mr Birk told me, 'This is where we have to effect certain fundamental and sartorial changes.' Taking a bulky sack he vanished inside. He had been wearing chalk stripe grey, blue-striped shirt with sep collar attached. He burst forth minutes later.

'Ricken we'll kitch t'ole hebb come mornin bor,' he said oddly. 'Git a nice ritch down t' awld river bor.' He was wearing huge thigh boots that caused him to walk with the rocking gait of a clockwork policeman. He had on an enormous gansy with unravelled sleeves and a horse-collar neck and over it a malodorous canvas smock that left red smears on everything it touched. On his head he wore a cloth cap gay with varnish, red lead and sump oil. The sweat was pouring down his face. He looked at my school blazer with its yellow and purple stripes, my grey flannel knickers and school cap with distaste. Snatching off my cap he ground it under his boot; he pulled out my shirt, yanked my blazer down over my shoulders and unzipped my fly. 'Put these on,' he commanded, producing a second pair of huge boots.

We rocked our way towards the creek heavily laden with baggage, ropes, bits of ironwork and homemade brawn in a string bag. I was carrying the repaired torpsul, authentically darned with genuine waxed flax by a traditional sailmaker. This man, Mr Birk told me, had lost an ear when fishing off the Winklesea Snorp. A conger eel got it when he was a lad. The mate had told him to bend over the open fish hold to look for the golden trunnel and 'Gor ee gannum smartish,' Mr Birk said.

I asked him shrewdly how he knew the conger was a young lad and why he was speaking in that odd manner. 'Mind your own damn business boy,' he said. He was carrying a new swifting thrank for the jumbo downhaul which the sailmaker had sold him for only fifty pounds. I thought it looked like a gardener's dibble. I had once seen our gardener's dibble.

Mr Birk used both oars to row us out but once we came into the view of the other people on the other gaffers, he rose unsteadily on his feet and, using only one oar and one hand, began splashing about over the stern thus moving us slowly along. There were two other gentlemen already aboard *Harvester*, one was unravelling his jumper and the other was painting his own trousers.

My nostrils flared to the sudden scent of rot, tar, fish and wet linoleum as we drew alongside. I grasped the bulwarks. The sheer beauty of the vessel – as in the case of a jobbing builder's backyard – was not immediately obvious, but I felt my pulse quicken and my eyes grow misty. Mr Birk was standing on my hands.

From gammon to fantail she was a credit to the shipwright's ancient art and I could imagine him hacking and hewing in drunken swipes while the fragrant pine chips flew, some of them two feet long to judge by the finish he had achieved. The mast and rigging soared aloft immaculate as a nightwatchman's greatcoat at a muddy dig. Something was stirring deep within me. I recalled Mummy's cream slices. But wait! Was this the beginning of the unhealthy craving Daddy had warned me about? I turned my thoughts to cold showers and Meccano.

Aboard, I was shown the shelf upon which I would sleep and given a locker, triangular in shape and full of beams, hard paint brushes and something wet in a sack. For supper we had pink and black sausages and many beans, which Mr Birk said was a portent of a fine wind tomorrow. Then our crew and those of the other gaffers all had to go ashore for a jug. To show willing I offered to go alone and collect all the jugs. Mr Birk was deeply moved, calling upon his Creator for strength.

We all went. It took a long time because we all had to stand up in our boats and using only one oar made us go in circles. We never did collect the jugs because we went to the Dog and Becket instead, where we drank beer. I had never tried beer. We sang 'Lo'stoff Sal is a big strong gal come up on me ole reef taykle O' and another song about Maggie Parsons' bloomers. I was taken seriously ill on the way back.

It was a hot, still night and, what with the genuine old bogey stove roaring and the oil lamps and the men's pipes all going so well, it became really cosy down below. They yarned under the cabin lamp. They discussed how spratt whifflers should be rigged. Mr Johnson said he liked little bumpkins but Mr Birk said they wring your fantail butts and spew oakum. They got me on deck just in time. We all slept with our shirts and caps on. When I went up on deck to be sick for the fifth time I was fortunate enough to witness the daily miracle of the dawn.

It was the day of the race. There was hardly any wind at first but we couldn't use our engine because we could not make the blowlamp work to heat the bulb. Astern of us was a restored cod banger which was fitted with an authentic 1908 cartridge start Blackstone. Mr Birk said that the owner, Old Harry, had no cartridges. 'Er course I tried to talk 'im outer usin' . . . Mr Birk began. There was a shattering roar, a yard of flame from her exhaust pipe and a swan fell dead. '. . . usin an Eley Kynoch number six cartridge,' Mr Birk finished.

Our trim little vessel still had her original rim-ram and randy wink. We hoisted the mainsail. It was like watching a camel getting to its feet and a shower of reddish dust fell on our heads. Mr Birk pointed out the wrinkles at the throat with approval. Mummy uses Oil of Ulay on hers. We hoisted torpsul and jib and dropped the mooring. There was a nice little breeze by then and our sails billowed out bravely as did those of the rest of the fleet. Mr Birk braced himself at the helm. For a long time our mooring buoys remained under our bows like whoopsies on a carpet.

God! but I shall never forget the thrill as, with roar of bow wave, rattle of hoops and rumble of rudder we thundered seawards. In less than half an hour our mooring buoys were almost out of sight astern.

The start was a classic. All five craft got away precisely on the second gun except for Mr Old Harry's cod banger which had a striped deckchair impaled on the bowsprit. On a nearby power cruiser my sharp scout's eyes noted an old gentleman with both legs in the air. The first mark lay a mile dead to windward but we fetched it in well under fifty tacks and leading the fleet by a biscuit's toss Mr Birk said. I tried it with a chocolate digestive. He made a strange sobbing noise.

I learned much about the science of racing that day. I had been given a responsible position sitting astride the very tip of the bowsprit, which Mr Birk said was the best place I could be for God's sake and the good of all aboard. Mr Birk did not like having to bear away when we were on port tack and my job was to yell out when I judged that I could gob down the neck of the other helmsman.

I was a proud lad out there and a target for all eyes. A chill wind set the peak of my school cap a'drumming and blew up the legs of my grey flannel knickers with a curious fluting sound which numbed my responses but little. Exhilarated I gave vent to the warbling cry of the whimbrel patrol. 'Wheeem–BRRRRILL,' I cried shrilly, bobbing my head characteristically. Close abeam to windward the helmsman of a bloater smack jerked round to listen, taking the tiller with him. As she fell astern with her jib aback he shouted out to me in a merry voice. 'Wheeem–BRRRRILL,'

I encored as we plunged past.

At the windward mark we bore off a full length ahead of all and it was there that Mr Birk scored his master stroke. While the rest of the fleet went tearing off on a broad reach for some totally different buoy in a most laughable manner, we were squared away on the final winning run – unstoppable, uncatchable.

We set a drabbler on our bonnet, a watersail below all, a jimmy green and a jib'o'jibs; then up went the fisherman jiggered on the boathook with the foresail wing-and-wing. It was still not enough for Mr Birk. Pulling out his shirt tail he spread it to the brawling wind. There wasn't a dry eye to be seen. On we raced, spars arcing, bag'o'wrinkle soughing. It was then that I knew I had failed Dad and Mum; that I had *fallen*, betrayed my young manhood, given my clean young mind to the *gaff*!

We crossed the line in solitary glory, taking the committee by surprise for no guns fired. Rounding up to our anchor with a rattle of shivs and a jangle of nips we brought up in a cloud of rust as the chain, dead flies and dog-ends roared out. I was still on the end of the bowsprit.

The other men went aft in solemn file and stood shoulder to shoulder facing astern, heads bowed in a moment of quiet thanksgiving. I did not disturb their reveries, but I knew with deep certainty that I was a man now and that I could hold my own with anybody.

I took to skippering the seventy-foot gaff schooner Hoshi *back in the early fifties when her owner 'Chunky' Duff was trying to make her pay her way by chartering. She was parish-rigged with pre-war sails and mainly sisal running gear and an engine that ran on equal proportions of oil, petrol and devout prayer. I had one inexperienced youth as mate and my rosary beads. Our clientele (paying crew we called them) had about as much nautical aptitude as the Little Sisters of the Poor and every cruise was akin to Columbus blundering off in search of a new world. That I never actually came to grief says much for my incredible good luck plus clean thoughts and cold showers.*

Let go!

Nowadays it would be called 'keeping a low profile'. How do you keep your profile low in seventy feet of battered gaff schooner which is emitting clouds of smoke from a cackling exhaust and which has a crew of novice paying guests, wearing flat caps and speckled sandshoes?

I did my best. I kept her aimed at the entrance to Cherbourg basin with my elbows tucked in and my collar turned up. Not good enough. There on the foredeck was Jock, my full-time mate. Jock was a repented Teddy Boy and he still had his regulation d.a. hair style, the full-drape coat with velvet collar, the tubular trousers and winkle picker shoes, all now whitened with salt water but striking none the less.

There were the occasions of earlier visits to remember. The last time we were there it was the little matter of our bowsprit and somebody's washing line; on another occasion it had been our man in his postman's cap (substitute for a yachting cap) and the sartorial perfection of the white-topped old gentleman on the neighbouring yacht

('What they charging you on your boat then mate?'). Then there was that other time and the heaving line delivered with devastating force at a point blank range of four foot six. And so on . . .

This time, I vowed, we'd do everything right. We would place our anchor exactly right and not so far out that we sagged, not so far in that we dragged, neither too much to windward nor leeward. There would be order and precision. There would be orders given quietly and executed smartly; a stern line taken ashore swiftly and secured correctly (I shuddered at a recollection and crossed myself). My voice would remain well modulated and I would *walk* forward to supervise the paying out of anchor cable. Yes I would.

Would I hell! Already the fates were sorting their marbles and the writing was on the wall – graffiti that was to haunt me all my days. Meanwhile I kept the shake out of my voice and addressed my lolling and unlikely crew in reasoned tones.

'We are going to motor into the basin and make a complete circuit,' I said. 'This will allow me to estimate exactly where to drop the anchor when we come round the second time. You all know your jobs. Jim and Olly will lower the boat and run the stern line ashore as I've explained, Fred and Shirley will stand by with fenders and the rest of you will sit down please and allow me a clear view ahead.'

They all nodded and to a man, got up and arranged themselves athwart the deck ahead as if about to field a notorious batsman.

'Jock,' I called, raising my voice just enough to reach the foredeck, like a lecturing guide in a cathedral, 'When I say Let Go, I want that anchor away smartly and on the bottom. Don't pay out any cable until you see us moving astern.' Jock nodded his vast forelock at me.

Nothing could go wrong. The boat was swung out in davits with a long warp faked and snaked ready to run, led aft outside all to our after bollard. The 200 lb Nicholson swung from the stemhead and we had ten fathoms ranged on deck. I turned my attentions to Jim and Olly. Total novices, but anglers, keen and lusty.

'Jim and Olly,' I said in the cooing tones a mother might use to her small daughter on the morn of her Holy Confirmation, 'When the time comes, lower smoothly together. Take your time. Then row quietly ashore and make fast.' I had a momentary vision of white veils and frilly knickers. I shook my head to clear it.

Then we were in the basin. That was in the days before the pontoon berths, when everybody laid to an anchor and moored stern to the quay wall. It was the post-war period of botched-up pre-war petrol auxiliaries, ex-WD gas capes in lieu of oilskins. It was a time when all the yachts in Cherbourg were usually British and the air was filled with the high toned fluting accents of the upper crust – with the stark exception of our lot . . .

'. . . And don't anybody *say* anything!' I added as a rider. I lined a distant shop front up with a bollard; just about right for my distance off next time round. I scouted about to find suitable cross marks. We were clipping along at a useful three knots. Jock was down on one knee as if waiting for the starter's gun; Jim and Olly were fiddling with the belayed falls of the dinghy, ready to lower smartly and efficiently. It flashed across my mind that I'd have been happier if Jock hadn't been holding the cable brake lever, and if Jim and Olly had had their great red fists stuck safely in their pockets when it happened . . .

I heard a squeal of blocks, a terrible oath from Olly and a rushing of water. 'OH GOD!' I screamed. Divine intervention had never been needed more.

Olly had let go the forward fall, the bow of the dinghy had plunged and she hung stern-uppards, filling with water. Jim was hanging on to the after fall staring at me in shock.

'LET GO MAN!' I roared.

And on the foredeck the words reached Jock's ears – which sent a message to his brain, which sent a message to his hand with carbon copy to knees and elbows. He jerked the lever and away went the anchor, at the run and speeded on its way by 50 tons of schooner doing three knots.

I danced. You read about it happening to people and it's true. I actually danced, I bounded up and down clawing the air, I hurled off my cap and I let out a shrill, pitiful keening cry eloquent of the sadness and suffering of all Mankind. My crew stared at me with wooden respect and not a little awe. They had paid good money to try this yachting lark and they were getting full value for it. Then speech returned to me, and I raked and rended them with a verbal broadside that extended three generations back and prophesied a dour future.

None of which helped. Jock had slammed the lever down and we brought up with a shuddering, metallic

squeal of links jumping the brake in a cloud of red dust and sparks. It shook every tooth in my head. The racket echoed round the basin, a 'Roll up, Roll up folks' signal that had every living thing gazing our way in pleased expectancy. Then our bows seemed to dip, she paused and she began to swing. Her fantail, seventy feet abaft her stem, swung in a scything sweep in amongst the anchored yachts, herding them into a heap like ewes, anchors dragging and tangling, owners up and cursing, wives trilling and waving fenders, dogs barking and Sleightholme hopping hither and yon babbling apologies and shoving the flat caps around as if trying to rearrange a bad stage set.

Oh the ignominy of it. When silence reigned again and we finally extricated ourselves, when I had bullied the last flat cap and croaked my final apology, arranged to pay for this and that and finally drawn off astern I felt empty – like a shriven sinner quitting the confessional and facing a monumental penance. We had still to berth the ship.

Round we went again, this time with every yacht in harbour lined with a glowering blood-hungry audience. You could feel the eyeballs swivelling, see the lips curling in fine scorn, hear the undertone of well-modulated honking, like a duckpond at dusk.

Round we came and this time I got it right. In other circumstances I would have been delighted to have an audience. It was perfect. The anchor went down exactly where I wanted it, the astern gear engaged smoothly and we began to haul astern neatly into the waiting berth. Away went Olly and Jim in the boat, stern line snaking out over the stern. What could possibly go wrong . . .?

Just one thing. Just one lousy, unforeseen, stupid thing. There they were, both sitting forward, dinghy stern in the air, oars splashing and flailing, boat zig-zagging and heading, not for the quayside but for the virgin topsides of the nearest neighbour yacht.

The owner seemed to be in some sort of trance. Then he jerked into action, interposing his body and a fender between the questing stem iron of the dinghy and his topsides. 'What in hell are you playing at?' he bellowed. 'Haven't you ever rowed a boat before man?'

'No,' said Jim and Olly in chorus, nodding their flat caps.

There are boats in which a flat battery would constitute a lifeboat emergency, their crews condemned to drift lost and in darkness, deprived of pump water, communication, microwave and the functioning of the loo. They would sit in helpless costive silence awaiting succour. 'Save the Battery' is the cry, as if it were some rare and threatened species. Yachts plug into the marina powersockets like suckling piglets, their dozen-and-one electronic dinkums peeping and tweeting, stereo blaring and a background of VHF mutter like eavesdropping outside a confessional. On less sophisticated vessels to leave the light on in the toilet is a crime of such breathtaking gravity that the owners brood for days, setting a good example by blundering around in there in the dark. Until the tip-up washbasin inadvertently tips up at a delicate moment. There comes an unearthly keening of distress.

The charge of the light brigade

The battery in the bilges is akin to an ailing relative with a bed in the front room downstairs.

'How's the battery?' we inquire solicitously.

Heads are shaken. 'The plates are hardening I'm afraid,' comes the depressing reply.

We tempt the invalid with distilled water and bang open the engine throttle with a generous hand. 'This'll do it some good,' we rejoice, scattering the sailboards. *Saving the battery* becomes a sort of conservationist cause as if it were an endangered species.

Many men seem to assume a sort of instinctive knowledge where electrics are concerned, a gift inherited from a host of shadowy ancestors rooting lethally in the cupboard under the stairs. As gifts go, it is about as helpful to your average DIY bungler as roll-on deodorant to a Whirling

Dervish. Armed with these genetic skills, father prowls the home. 'I've just had a look at your washing machine,' he tells his wife, as if his basilisk eye was all that was necessary. 'It'll be goodbye collar grime and troublesome egg stains from now on,' he chuckles as he switches on. The machine shudders, emits a warning puff of blue smoke and then takes off like a Harrier Jet.

And take fixing the Christmas tree lights. A sedan chair on the Hammersmith Flyover offers occupant and bearers more promise of peace and holy quiet than the festive tree rocking in its bucket. Humming his harsh little tune, he juggles with dud bulbs, and the family, keeping its distance, awaits the inevitable howling denunciation of bad workmanship, the scuttling cat, a clip round the ear and half the floorboards up.

Aboard his boat his talents can be given full rein. 'Right then,' he warns, stuffing wires into a fusebox like a robin nesting in a gardener's boot, 'SWITCH ON!' Up in the forespeak his wife presses the switch.

'Nothing!' she cries triumphantly.

He can't understand it. 'I can't understand it,' he wails, truthfully. Then comes the fuse-in-fuse-out, you-switch-on-when-I-say-NOW routine. By the time it is discovered that the switch was upside-down, tempers are as raw as a flint-knapper's thumb.

For a man whose progress about the house can be tracked by the lights left blazing in his wake, his concern for the state of the battery aboard is matched only by that of the naturist for the state of his bowels. At the best of times (like following six hours of harrowing flat-out motoring against a spring ebb off Ushant) he is parsimonious about battery use. 'Why? I can still see perfectly well,' he lies pressing nose to printed page. Your lonely crofter examining the latest Damart catalogue (delivered across six miles of wind-swept grouse moor by a cursing postman) gets a better light from his tallow dip than the average saloon on a rainy evening, when grey gloom is transformed magically to a yellowish one at the flick of a switch. The alternative, the overhead fluorescent strip light, renders haggard the daintiest cheek and creates the uncanny illusion that those sitting hollow cheeked in its baleful light have just quit Shangri-La in a hurry.

Looking at the battery, a ceremony implying hushed and private worship, is ritualistically timed to take place during that supper time interval between straining rice for the packet paella and getting everybody to sit down *for God's sake*. With his huge and straining denim bum stuck up like a dolmen over the gaping hole in the floorboards, people are left to manoeuvre around it as if competing in some curious dressage event. He consults his hydrometer and sighs draughtily. Mother studies his rump without love and, grim-lipped, gets the oil lamp out.

The hydrometer is his badge of office. Resembling some part of a comic doctor sketch this huge syringe contains a gaily coloured float which, when the battery is fully charged, leaps to its feet in a military manner, or lolls upwards drunkenly for a half charge, or (usually) half rises and then sinks back wearily like a husband at table acknowledging the arrival of lady guests. According to this dreary little repertoire, the ship's company mourns or rejoices, uses the light in the heads, or thuds and curses its way into sleeping bags in total darkness. The wind generator, a sort of Phyllosan for ageing batteries, has brought a new dimension to the game and no longer does a howling windy night hold father in dread. The black squall that has laid waste the runner beans across four counties brings him chuckling from his bunk, hydrometer in hand, as his windmill thumps in milliamps like ants scuttling into a hollow log.

Old Harry was late to discover the boon of the switch. His first electrification plant included a massive dynamo with cast iron feet like a Victorian bath, belt-driven by his rocking Kelvin. No batteries were involved. His navigation lights waxed and waned according to the urgency of the manoeuvre, thus haunting harbour masters and enlivening the dull monotony of many a ship's bridge. Then came the huge bank of Leyden jars (misleadingly labelled 'Thompson's Olde Fashioned Pickles'), which popped and bubbled like some exhibits in a grisly pathological museum. These were succeeded in due course by a pair of conventional heavy duties, courtesy of a wrathful Dutch lorry driver marooned in a lay-by near Strood. Antlered with crocodile clips like the Stag At Bay they sprouted a tangle of drooping leads as if gingered by some astonishing garden fertiliser.

The design and construction of a wind generator posed no problems. The first model, utilising six cricket bats (courtesy of Church lads Sports and Social club), adzed to a more acceptable aerodynamic shape, was set up in the form of a test rig in his backyard – a wise precaution and an instant success as the flashing blades dissolved into a drumming disc of naked power. The postman, veteran of a score of bitterly offended bull terriers, wandered in through the gate. The Damart catalogue he was studying featured a bevy of young women laughing sardonically at each other's knickers, guests perhaps at some bizarre cocktail party for the absent-minded. The whirling blades Black-and-Deckered off the peak of his cap and hit him squarely in his assorted circulars, a catastrophe that sent him whooping off up the street with the great bounds of a moon-walking astronaut.

Learning much from this dummy run, our inventor then tried a variety of windmills on board his vessel in both the vertical and the horizontal planes, which shucked the buttons off club blazers or brought down showers of seagull feathers according to location alow or aloft. The final site at the end of the bowsprit provided a safe position where the device could scream and judder without threat to the human frame. It was a pity that Old Harry decided to manoeuvre bows first into the town marina.

On the catwalk ahead there stood the lady MP, a prominent figure noted for her outstanding manifestos. She was wearing a pork-pie hat, twisted stockings and a knitted jumper suit that made her look like Richard the Lionheart in flat heels. She stopped to pat a cornered child and there was this loose strand of wool . . . 'Catch a turn forr'd,' ordered Old Harry, intent upon his ancient art, 'Surge handsome and get it off her!'

Within seconds, and snared by those deadly blades, she was spinning and jigging in a spirited tarantella, her woolly pupa unravelling until she was reduced to a bare complexity of sturdy backstays and swifters, rigged down for winter North Atlantic and corsetted like some gigantic armadillo. With a roar that was once the pride of the hustings, she hurled her handbag. This vast reticule, the size and weight of a plumber's toolbox, hit Old Harry between wind and water, wrenching from him a diaphonic grunt that alerted the Coastguards from Hull to the Watford Gap.

I have never been much of a ladies' man. As a youth I was spotty as a set of dominoes, my trousers were always too short and my jackets hung round my skinny neck like a horse collar. I have managed the odd nocturnal scuffle but never much by way of meaningful relationships. There was one short, fat girl I went steady with for the whole of one summer but what with my lankiness and her squatness, all we needed was baggy pants, stepladders and a pail of whitewash and any circus would have been glad to engage us.

Things broke up one hot summer's evening at the pictures. Just before 'picking her up' at the bus stop (it would have taken a better pair of biceps than mine) I had been wrestling with an escaped billy goat that was loose in our garden. I was wearing my mid-calf flannels and a Harris tweed jacket which had never been nearer the Western Isles than the Watford Gap, the billy goat wore racing handlebars and a caftan of reeking brown shag. We'd been sitting in the hot cinema for about half an hour before the miasma of randy goat began to rise from me in shimmering waves. Explanations didn't help. 'I'm sorry,' she said, lumbering to her feet, 'but if nobody else will tell you, then I will!'

Muck, mud and Gladys

My yachting career stretches astern in an unbroken line of muddy footprints, a smacking and slithering gait spanning the years. I first went afloat at the age of five, not, as one would suppose, in the care of some indulgent uncle, but in the muck-yard of a Lincolnshire farm and under the sceptical eyes of a raddled old hen and a horse. It was that sort of farm, a menagerie of banging corrugated iron, barren cows and Grandad with string round his ankles to defeat climbing mice – which they knew was hopeless anyway in view of his impregnable flannel combinations.

My Godmother visited us, bringing a parcel each for me and my sister. Mine was a knobbly parcel, and hers yielded up a beautiful doll, all smirk and knicker, which upon being lifted from its box opened its eyes with the painful reluctance of a rugby supporter the morning after the dinner. I retired under the table to open mine – a retreat made private by a floor-length tablecloth – and ripping off the brown paper I stared with numb outrage at what I found. It was as if Hamlet's skull had flipped open and begun to play a tune. I drew a long, slow, deep breath while my face crinkled up and changed from dental-pink through magenta to bed-jacket purple; then I let out a brassy bellow of fury causing my mum to blow a mouthful of tea half across the room. What I had found in my parcel was a pair of black boots and on the back of each was a tab bearing the misleading legend 'Little Gents'.

It was embarrassment all round. Flushed out with the kitchen brush, my feet were rammed into the Little Gents and I was hustled outside, still bellowing, to play like a good boy, clattering off to find my destiny afloat with a kick at the cat as I went. It had been a wet winter and the only drain in the muck-yard had long since become blocked, so that the place was awash with a sea of reeking ordure to which pigs, cows and horses had contributed with the liberality of donors to a good cause. The colour of the stuff was indescribable, but the scientifically-minded reader, if so inclined, could achieve a fair likeness by boiling a child's paintbox in a gallon of senna. Half-afloat there lay a stable door. My howls died away as my mind grappled with an idea, then grunting I launched it fully.

I shall never forget that momentary magic, that sensation of being afloat, of an up-thrusting, shifting, yielding, yet buoyant platform, and I stood beaming around in my short-lived triumph. Then it sank. It went down quite slowly and the tide of foulness lipped and lapped up and then over the tops of my Little Gents, filling them and creeping up my ankles to my knees. For the second time inside ten minutes I let fly with a howl of impotent fury and frustration.

It was some years before I bettered that promising start and we had moved to Hull where the mud of the Humber foreshore had a magnetic fluidity that drew me like Jason to the Golden Fleece. There was me, Betty and Derek, and a hulk with a rotting gangplank. Betty was aged ten and almost incandescent with exploding puberty. 'If you and me went into the bushes you could teach me how to wrestle,' she said, sidling up close. I hooted with mirth. 'What! Me wrestle with a *girl*,' I choked, *'wrestle with girls!'* Still overcome by this absurd notion and laughing with scorn I went bounding up the gangplank. Derek and Betty went bounding off for a wrestle. My gangplank broke.

I reached teenage via the mud of Barnstaple, the upper reaches of Newton Abbot and then Wootton Creek on the Isle of Wight. I was a shy youth, tall, cavernously narrow and with ribs like an African xylophone, my elbows and knees like Meccano parts and being a boy scout, spending long hours on hands and knees puffing at camp fires, my eyes were almost permanently red-rimmed, like those of an ornamental pheasant. My first date with a girl was a blind one set up for me by my friend Murray. His date arrived first that summer evening at our rendezvous by the seashore (which is the only nautical connection with this incident) and of course she was a stunner, ash-blonde, slender and with a fo'c'sle you could balance a jug on. 'Gladys is just behind,' she said inaccurately. Gladys wasn't, we noted. Gladys was shaped like a glue kettle with the neck of a Turkish wrestler and lugging a handbag that should have been on a golf trolley.

Murray led the way with his date tripping along laughing gaily, while we followed in an aching silence like prisoner and escort. Ahead, on the brink of the woods, which were our inevitable goal, I saw Murray pause at a boggy patch and, swinging his giggling companion up into his arms, he strode manfully and skilfully past the mire and off into the gloom. We reached the boggy patch. 'Ah,' I said, 'Well now, ah!' She had stopped, shifted her handbag and assumed a half-crouch. She looked at me expectantly. With my grin frozen like a Greek mask I strove for a purchase around her waist, grabbing a reliable hold of coat and muscle, while my other hand dug down for a grip behind her knees. I braced myself and heaved. It was like trying to lift a tar-boiler. I stifled a tortured grunt as my arms shuddered with strain and my mouth twitched with effort, but I got her airborne and stood there swaying, while she screeched with delight and flailed about with her handbag.

I took one step forward, then brought the other leg up. All at once I began to sink smoothly into the soft earth, going down like a cinema organist and in panic I struggled to extract one foot, only to overbalance. We crashed to the ground like a collapsing warehouse, sprawling forward into the mire. That was the end of our romantic tryst. I levered myself slowly and drippingly erect, and gave vent to a single, forbidden and socially inexcusable expletive. 'There are *ladies* present,' Gladys said in awful tones. I apologised through clenched teeth. 'I think I'd better take you back,' I told her. It made her sound like a faulty lampshade.

Had I been younger and lovelier I might well have enjoyed windsurfing but it all came about long after the spring had left my stride and the blossom of my youth had turned to compost. Nowadays if I were to wear a wet-suit it would look like a Christmas stocking full of walnuts and oranges. I once had a go on my granddaughter's surf board. I floundered shorewards panting and haggard, watched carefully by a part-time lifeguard who plainly contemplated the prospect of administering mouth-to-mouth with little pleasure.

Centre of effort

There was a time when your seaside boarder wore either worsted trousers and a flat cap or a cameo brooch and twisted stockings. Your old-time landlady, dusting off the pork loaf and heating the sandwich curlers would have detonated her modesty front* had she been confronted by one of today's boarders. At the sight of him battling his way in through the bead curtain with his 15ft plank and felling the Stag at Bay with one sweep of his back-pack she would have lost her aplomb and revealed her foibles.

Sailboarding has done for the dignity of seafaring what the celluloid dicky did for the Edwardian after dinner speaker. No acrobat in wrinkled tights ever flattened a human pyramid to more riotous applause than your brandy raconteur with his dicky alight. The tyro sailboarder, buttocks stuck out like a cake trolley as he wobbles into the path of the Cowes ferry, elicits much the same good natured gust of appreciative laughter from her Captain.

A total disregard for the Rules of the Road gives the

*Modesty Front: a sort of frilly dodger worn up front by landladies to counter inflation.

sailboarder a place in maritime society akin to that of the paint-by-numbers artist at the Tate Gallery. Father, newly in possession of his Yachtmaster Certificate – the seatime for which was painfully acquired, huddled waxen-faced in the corner of any cockpit that would have him – views these flights of swerving, collapsing, dithering aquabatics with a sense of outrage. The long and yawning hours at the Evening Institute watching a venerable Master Mariner with egg on his collar and an unzipped fly draw squeaky right-of-way diagrams on the blackboard has left him as eager to practise his new skills as your fledgling blackbird poised on the edge of the nest above the water butt.

'I've got right of way!' he shrills. The hurtling boarder, a first-time plasterer's mate from Brixton, rockets across the bows and straight up the beach, flattening sandcastles en route for an unexpected tryst with a massive matron who is changing under a heaving back towel into her 'Knit-this-figure-flattering-two-piece-for-the-fuller-figure-in-rugwool-on-big-needles swim-suit'!

The pleasures of scaring the ghost out of pedalo riders and reducing Trinity House Pilots to a state of thumb-sucking shock, curled up in a foetal ball under the radar display, soon palls for the boarder and he seeks fresh outlets for his skill. Wearing his expression of wooden nonchalance bordering upon boredom he demonstrates freestyle and reverse rail-ride for the benefit of cursing and dodging cruising yachtsmen. Far downriver a *YM* reader, unsuccessful author of ten rejected cruising yarns, is rowing thoughtfully shorewards. He is composing yet another opening paragraph. 'The ebb bubbled over the cobbles,' he tries, mouthing it experimentally. 'The ebb shimmered over the shallows, gurgled past the groynes, dimpled past the dunes . . .' The boarder, going backwards with legs crossed, hits the author square in the port rowlock. '. . . gargled under the garboards . . .' finishes our reader sinking from view. The ideal, we are told, is to carry a board on deck while cruising, where it is as handy as a piano accordion in a phone booth but giving pleasure to both young and old and reducing the stentorian roars of Roy-

46

al Harbourmasters to meadow-pipit squeaks. It might, in time, replace the conventional tender. One can visualise a joyless little queue of mum with headscarf and string bag in transit with dad, the kids and cousin Percy ('We've simply *got* to invite him sometime') proceeding shorewards like paper-hangers on a wobbly trestle.

Schools for teaching the art proliferate. The undeviating course of the tyro, like moth to candle, is bright with the promise of spectacular mayhem. 'We manoeuvre,' says the instructor to a portly lady student with a figure like a stack of scatter cushions, 'by shifting our weight.' With

her board safely beached she does so. It creaks. 'Now flex the knees and sway the trunk, letting your Centre of Effort move aft . . .' She does so, assuming the wary stance of a wicket-keeper facing a demon bowler and an absentminded old gentleman towing a hall hat stand on a dog lead taps out his pipe in passing.

Your Proper Cruising Yachtsman, dedicated to anchoring in places shunned by everybody else, cannot expect to avoid the boarder for long. Anchored so far up an unmapped creek that he is liable for local Rates, he gathers his sighing family close. 'If we keep quiet, very quiet,' he says in hushed tones, 'we may – just *may* be lucky enough to hear the mating call of the Little Sidebinder!' Stunned by the promise of so rare a treat nobody notices the approach of the boarder. Engrossed in the tricky exercise of standing on one leg with his elbow in his mouth he is oblivious to the network of kedge lines and tripping lines that surround the cruiser. His board knifes under a warp. He takes to the air with an eerie, warbling cry. 'The male!' shouts father in triumph. 'Now let's see if it has the typical purple rump.'

The first time Old Harry saw a boarder in action he was moved to an act of unselfish generosity so typical of the man. 'Why dog-bite-me it's scandalous the work riggers do these days,' he observed, watching the boarder struggle to hold up his colourful rig. 'That pore feller needs a bit o' seven-by-nine and a couple of deadeyes. Now I'm not promising nothing but maybe we could fix him up.' So saying he bore off hard in pursuit, his bowsprit pointing at the now cringing boarder with the damned accusation of Lord Kitchener's finger. 'Hold yore luff an' I'll be along of you,' Old Harry promised. Cheered by this prospect the boarder luffed frantically shorewards. The cranse iron took him between the shoulder straps and bore him aloft, little black legs pedalling furiously, like a beetle on a pin.

Upon realising the nature of the problem Old Harry at once saw scope for improving the sailboard design and set to work on a version of his own. Comprising a duck punt and the complete rig from his converted mussel-drubbler the board was an instant and predictable success.

Scorning the complications posed by a foul looking dusk and a rising wind he prepared for a test run. 'Now don't let go until I nod my head,' he told his keen helper. 'Nod your head?' the fellow queried, seeking confirmation. Old Harry nodded.

The story will long be related in chimney corners of how an apparition appeared – *not of this earth* – flying low over the water like some monstrous bat of Nordic folklore. In a wet suit cleverly adapted from an old suit of Long Johns generously coated with black varnish he took on a satanical appearance, enhanced by his sepulchral wailing as he sped upriver in the gloaming.

Meanwhile, back at the clubhouse it was AGM night. The Chairman had just asked for a show of hands – a foolhardy request at fitting out time – when Old Harry hit the club jetty. Quitting his board with legs moving in a blur of speed his impetus carried him onwards, barrelling clubwards, Nemesis in sandshoes.

'Any other business then?' asked the Chairman anxious to be off. An out-of-town member with transparent ears and a throat like a washbasin wastepipe was on his feet in a flash with finger upraised. He only had a small motion.

'Mister Chairman, I would like to move . . .' he got out. Then, still carrying his sail like a protest banner and going like a runaway tarboiler, Old Harry burst in through the end door on drumming feet and caught the member square on. The hellish impact carried the whooping delegate up the centre aisle to where the Chairman – not a well man at the best of times – stood with sagging jaw.

It has been said by reliable witnesses that the final crash not only flattened his lectern but activated the sprinkler system, drove the caretaker's muzzle deep into his Pot-Noodle and caused a warlike Ward Sister in a nearby clinic to cut herself shaving.

I once attended a day-course on the care and welfare of marine engines, a sort of pre-natal clinic for half-wits delivered by a diesel midwife in a Volvo boilersuit who dealt minutely with the mechanical equivalents of colic and breastfeeding. It left me slightly dazed, in possession of a stack of leaflets but little the wiser. Still, I can dip my sump, bleed my airlock and change my impeller but it is the total sum of my obstetrical knowledge of engines. A lifetime of owning boats with geriatric engines has left me thankful for small mercies and when mine starts, albeit with the coughing and grunting of an old man waking to a new day, I am filled with wonder, gratitude and wary optimism.

Don't choke her

I have only once owned a brand-new boat with a brand-new engine and even that machine had its fancies. It didn't fancy swing or lifting bridges, lock gates (closed), marina berths with boats unexpectedly backing out from them and people who said, 'Quick, start the engine'. Otherwise it gave good service. My other boats, owned or under my charge, all had machines in them that had either been something else in a previous incarnation or *should* have been something else – like a mooring block.

There was a certain ancient diesel. A strong man, well nourished and rested, in the full flower of manhood could *just* manage to start that machine. To have fitted an electric start would have called for a shore power line and blacking out half the county. It needed two of you, one to crank and the other playing the decompression cocks like a cinema organist. The crank man would limber up, hyperventilate, cross himself, flex his fingers and go to it. With the cocks open it would go; chuff ... suck ... chuff ... suck, chuff, suck, chuffsuck, chussuk, chussukchussukchussuk – then the athlete, with face scarlet and teeth clenched would nod his head and the cocks would be closed. If it fired you were OK; if it didn't, your athlete was finished, done, an empty bag. He couldn't manage a second go and you'd lead in the next athlete. That engine would have made a good Olympic event.

Then there was the launch with that dear old 10 hp petrol Brit, drip-lubrication like Mother Shipton's well and a flywheel like the Rank gong. When she was running she just sat there on her bearers shaking with mirth like a shop-window Father Christmas, but she was a fussy old starter on cold mornings, due perhaps to the valve tappet shims cut from cornflake packet or Shredded Wheat card according to the diet of the day.

All hands save the starter man would crowd forward into the bows until the propeller was out of the water. She had no clutch; you were either going or stopped and to stop her you removed a certain wire, albeit gingerly. The starter man would begin cranking in a series of grunting jerks while the watchers began the ritual of sympathetic curses or encouragement. 'Ah,' we would chorus if the engine coughed, or 'Nearly!' or 'Don't choke her!' – the latter a plea for clemency rather than mechanical advice. Then she would burst into action with a stupendous rattle and a fan of spray would rise from under the stern. 'ALL AFT,' the starter man would yell and we'd bound sternwards. The propeller would bite and the shuddering would cease. Conversation would be resumed where it had been left off prior to the procedure.

There was a 4-horse Stuart that almost sank me. It was a flat calm and I had my big ghoster set and sheeted home; I was alone and the ebb was due to start, which was like standing at the foot of the wrong escalator. I needed the engine.

It was a hot, sultry day with big ominous clouds building. Cranking fruitlessly below I was building a big, ominous temper and didn't observe the swag-bellied cumulonimbs squatting on the near horizon. I had reached the bit

51

where you stand at the gas stove holding the plug in a pair of pliers (having pencilled your points and other cabalistic rituals), when I heard a sound like the rushing of many wings. 'Birds,' I thought, wildly mistaken. The 'birds' hit us square on with hail, rain and spray in a devastating single blast of wind. The 5-tonner went down flat like a bit of banana-skin comedy and the sea poured in over the lee cockpit coaming. She just lay there, filling, rudder out of the water and me out of the cabin as if assisted by exploding trousers. I clung to the weather sheet winch with my lower half immersed and there wasn't a damn thing I could do until, belatedly, I remembered the main sheet. It too was under water but I slipped it and up we came. I had the cabin sole awash halfway up the bunks and by then a steady Force 6 blowing. From then on I was hopping around like a fiddler's elbow trying to reef, pump, miss the Maplins and wring out my trousers. The Stuart, plugless, crouched in its kennel forgotten.

I should by now be a little old wizard with engines but sadly I'm not. Anything with more moving parts than a clockwork Noddy has me beaten. I have a rough idea of what is going on in my engine and I can ascribe meanings to some of the rattles and thuds it produces, but only in the manner of a man listening to noisy neighbours through the party wall. I know enough maintenance-manual jargon to be able to silence my wife with science when she gets uppity about failures to start, engage, reverse, tendencies to stop, falter, or make rasping noises. She once defeated me though and this gives her an edge. It was one of the non-starting occasions and I had tried everything from bleeding the line to fanning it with my cap. I would have lit a candle to Saint Peter if it hadn't been for the fumes.

'The last time it started, the forehatch was open,' she said critically. I fell about with derisive laughter, I gave her a look of withering, pitying contempt but I felt an icy clutch of foreboding.

'Try it,' she said, as I'd known she would. I argued, sneered, rolled my eyes and called upon my Maker to witness her stupidity. Well, you can guess what happened, can't you? She opened the forehatch, I swung the handle and that engine sang into action as if it had never been silent.

I once had a cut-out switch mounted upside down. It was mounted that way because having spent twenty minutes poking bits of wire into the back of a panel, and finally hit target and screwed up I was damned if I'd go through it all again just because the switch happened to be base over apex. It cost me a yard engineer's wages for

two hours before he tumbled it. My wiring systems tend to be a bit like that. They are sound and they work but they look like a magician's workshop and all they lack is Frankenstein rising from his bed of terminals and switches. It is the first start of the season that poses the problems, because by then I've forgotten what goes where.

I once had a little gaff cutter with a pre-war Morris from some long defunct motor-car. It had been marinised by a madman of limited ability and still fewer tools; the original gearbox had been blanked off in some fashion so that you shoved your handle forward to go astern and aft to go ahead. You primed the water pump via a priming cock on top of the block, closing it smartly the instant a jet of rusty water shot past your ear. The throttle consisted of a threaded rod of great length and a nut which had to be twiddled with great rapidity in a tight spot; string operated the choke and the gearbox was a crash one. In motion the whole thing sounded like a truck load of empty bean cans rolling down a tin roof; it shook, spat, backfired and clattered in maniacal fury. Every spring, Keith would come down and start it for me.

The first start of the year was ceremonial, like wassailing the apple trees. He would arrive with a small but amazingly heavy bag of tools. My job was to stand to one side looking helpful. I frowned when he frowned, clucked when he did and peered, bent, sidestepped and intoned after him like some altar boy assisting at a strange mechanical Mass.

Some engines start hesitantly, like a nervous public speaker; others, after a long period of cranking, fiddling and experimental adjustment, explode into full life like dynamiting a factory chimney. This engine was one of those. We were in a sort of marina; just enough water in the drying berth to feed the cooling intake, and it was one of those silent, still, holy-feeling Sunday mornings when people were either in bed, in church or bending over rusty mechanical relics. Keith had gone through all the preliminaries. He took hold of the starting handle without much optimism. By rights there should have been an hour of sweating and cursing ahead of him with me saying, 'She fired!' every time there was a chuffing sound. Not a bit of it. With everything full open that engine blasted into motion on the first jerk.

The metallic scream echoed off the hills, dogs barked, seagulls rose screaming and at full chat it blasted peace to smithereens. Aground, the vibration was horrific. I saw three of everything at once. I could feel my jowls flapping. From the galley there came a sympathetic tintinnabulation of pans, mugs and bottles, the forehatch slammed shut and lockers fell open. Keith was leaping and yelling, trying to stop it. The blast of rusty water had got him square and the cooling outlet was throwing a jet of dead spiders and rusty water clean into the next berth but one. It wouldn't stop. I, white faced and craven, had dived for cover but he, a man of sturdy stuff, fell upon the plug leads tugging frenziedly and howling and cursing as the shocks ran through him. It stopped. It was two hours before it would start again.

There was also this big old petrol Gray that muttered; it was like listening outside a confessional. You'd be going along trying to navigate or carry on a conversation and all the time you'd have one ear cocked for trouble. You made repeated trips to the side to see if cooling water was coming out and even today, starting my car, I have to resist the urge to wind down and peer out. When the water stopped you saw steam and you knew that you had about three minutes to find somewhere to anchor. It was like musical chairs. Once that engine was hot – even a bit warm – nothing would start it again and starting cold you had to kneel sideways and jerk savagely like fishing something nasty out from under a hedge.

There was an Elto outboard bought for two quid in 1938 which would run in a water butt, and a tarted up Morris Minor that I winterised with varnish in mistake for oil (it was a dark shed). I was an uneasy shipmate with a petrol-paraffin Parsons older than sin that ran a hot shaft bearing, brewed up some oily rags and inspired gallantry in all. We hauled the engineer out by his ankles after the skipper had donged him with a fire extinguisher, which was empty in any case.

Starting procedures are all different. To my shame, how often I have written that bit about 'teaching all the family how to start your engine'. With my present one you'd need a weekend seminar. On fuel, choke open, throttle advanced to first rusty mark, turn over with switch off, turn over with switch on. Then, *if* she fires, in choke, open and make wowing noise with throttle, open exhaust cooler cock *seven* turns. By which time the swing bridge has closed again.

*Yachting journalists grow accustomed to the sort of launching
parties where the promoters of a new class, hungry for free
publicity, lash out the supermarket champagne and run amok
with cheese fingers and bits of tinned pineapple impaled on
toothpicks. The hack, nursing the secret that the event is only
worth two 3-column inches of 8-point and a much-reduced
photo, munches in the biting east wind. He claps perfunctorily
as the boat-lift waddles down the slip with its flag-bedecked
burden while he calculates how soon he can get the hell out of
it without being noticed.*

*I once watched this sort of launch of a huge, amateur-built
ferro-cement ketch owned by a syndicate of wheat-germ
munching weirdos who planned to sail around the world. They
never got further than Lymington where the profusion of writs
nailed to the mast gave it the festive appearance of a frilled
lamb chop. At the launch and due to a wild error in ballasting
she floated high as a dead dog and with the same degree of
stability. The guests flocked aboard, she lolled steeply to port,
then to starboard as they panicked shorewards.
Photographically it was the Picture of the Year, had I
remembered to take off my lens cap.*

Many a slip . . .

A launching party can be anything from two men and a
dog standing in the rain waiting for the tide to rise (it cuts
by six inches that day) to the full rich pageantry of proper
ceremonial. White clouds bowl in splendour across ceru-
lean skies and the whole yard is *en fête*. Spotless tablecloths
flutter, bunting crackles in the breeze, pennants snap and
wave . . . the yard chippy studies the ceremonial launching platform with canny misgiving. Built by a jug-eared
apprentice with more acne than acumen, its grinding

scarf joints grin evilly under the cover of bedraped flags. 'Come on, everybody up,' carols the happy owner leading the way up the ominously creaking ladder. 'Three rousing cheers and *down* she'll go . . .'

A launching party in March offers rich opportunity for truly memorable misery. Standing in a bleak and withering blast of drizzle, guests with faces mottled like boarding house linoleum, owlish from champagne and with smiles that look as though they have been painted on, wait while the yard foreman below struggles to free a jammed roller. His best blue suit is dappled with mud like a pantomime horse and he is cursing in a bitter and unrepetitive monotone. The owner's wife clutches the beribboned bottle with warlike intent. She is wearing a grey trouser suit that looks from the rear like a tourist's snap of the Arc de Triomphe. She is rehearsing *sotto voce*, the moment is at hand; the yacht is to be named *Nitty Gritty.*

'Ay neem ha . . . Gritty ti . . .' She pauses. 'Titty Gritty,' she improves. The freeing of the roller is followed by her Herculean but delayed swipe. Missing, she spins like a forklift truck and lams into the waistcoat of the alderman behind her. The breath whistles out of him like a deflating Avon.

Now and again the Press are invited. A yacht is being sponsored by a manufacturer of essential toiletry to set up yet another round-the-world record (sailed by the first oldest student on an Arts Council grant still having all his own teeth) to celebrate the 28,000th mile of Jumbotex tissue. The yacht designer, haggard with suspense, considers his designed waterline with glum foreknowledge like a birthday party juggler eyeing the small boy with a water pistol. An invited celebrity, now blasted half out of his skull on pre-launch drinks, advances with rolling eye to declare the new wing open and exhorts all to give freely.

Munching steadily between gulps, the journalists view the stirring ceremony with old, sad eyes and an *Observer* photographer takes a low angle shot of the Chairman's nostrils against a background of smoking chimneys.

'Toilet role for tax-fiddle Superyacht,' writes the *Daily Grind* man. 'Fifty-year-old, balding £60,000-a-year double divorcee Norman Sminge, Chairman of twice-liquidated Joyroll Holdings Ltd, launches playboy toy . . .' The yachting journalists, innocent as Miss Muffet in Toyland, scribble busily about aspect ratios.

Trying to do the job on the cheap is putting the roller skate on the top step. Or to lob in another metaphor; it isn't yodelling up the chimney but staying to listen for the echo that brings the soot down. With a bottle of Babycham for the lorry driver and two quid to the crane man in his dinner hour, the scene is set as inevitably as weak elastic in the Prize Day Mums' Sack Race. (Somebody called out 'Nicolas' and she jumped to conclusions.)

The owner looks at the kinked and bristling wire slings and re-reads his insurance policy in blind panic. 'I only hope that I'll be properly covered!' he squeaks. His yacht bounces aloft. A torrent of dirty rainwater gushes down from a scupper.

There may also be a spiteful little onshore wind with waves slapping the jetty like cynical applause. He watches, white knuckled, his stomach like turnips in a string bag. The crane operator, who needs no crystal ball to reckon up the odds, advises stepping the mast before she goes in; he has a bucket of black filth ready to hand for smearing on those parts of mast and rigging which his wire may fail to daub. The owner considers this suggestion. 'I think I'd rather step in the water,' he opts, walking backwards, keenly watched by the driver.

With a boat jerking and plunging alongside, stepping a mast is like trying to spear the last olive in the bottle with a short cocktail stick. The owner, hugging the foot of his mast, dances prettily to and fro, treading a saucy measure betwixt coachroof and foredeck. 'Let me give you a' ninch,' offers the crane driver. Down comes the butt as up comes the deck. Later, all damages dealt with, the owner will have to explain to many a frowning bystander why he has a fairy ring of mushroom ventilators dotted at random around the foot of the mast.

When Old Harry relaunched his rebuilt, lengthened, converted Polperro Snogger, no expense was spared. From his site behind the Quality Pork Butcher (Gentry our speciality) he laid down ways heavily-coated with a foul compound boiled up in advance, the stench of which had caused the drains to be ripped up throughout the Parish and tuppence on the rates. It must be admitted that the slope was somewhat steeper than the declivity normally favoured in less advanced shipyards and the creek at that point was perhaps a shade narrower than absolute perfection might have required, but Old Harry had allowed for all this. His complex calculations could be seen chalked on every last inch of available wall. An elderly gentleman, beset by the demands of nature, paused to study the brickwork and walked off carrying vital computations of weight and velocity.

On the day of days, correctly attired in a morning suit loaned for the morning by a dry cleaner against its owner's return, he advanced carrying his maul to where the one last remaining shore stood quivering with strain. A poignant moment. He paused, maul uplifted. There was a lump in his throat which his borrowed bowtie rode like a trip-switch. 'I'm sorry,' he apologised in a choking voice not entirely attributable to emotion, 'sometimes I get carried away . . .'

Down came the maul. With a rumble she was at him. Howling he leapt high, smacking a firm grip around the bowsprit and like some ancient classical figurehead he was borne pedalling furiously to his watery destiny.

Across the river lay the latest SkiHi power cruiser with a towering chromium howdah, more windows than Harrods and a double bed with legs like a hockey mistress. The Snogger, bows up and planing, carried its whooping burden across the creek with the accuracy of a sniper's bullet. Old Harry, legs extended wide, looked like some Olympic gymnast who had missed the bar and was set fair to dash his aspirations on the vaulting horse.

The power boat owner with Bermuda shorts and firm underlying principles was oblivious to the menace without. Head stuck deep in the radar hood, one hand holding his manual and the other twiddling his display he stooped to his task.

'Aha!' he rejoiced prematurely. 'Here comes a strong little signal. . .'

I never enjoy being on committees yet I seem to get on them without really trying. You should really avoid AGMs, which is when last year's committee retires, briefly, and when fresh blood may be sought. The Chairman is like a witch doctor smelling out evil-doers, 'Come on now, surely one of you will volunteer?' he wheedles. We all sit there on buttock-racking plastic chairs, avoiding his eye. I begin reading the instructions on a nearby fire extinguisher. Direct at seat of blaze, *it tells me usefully. 'There must be someone . . .' he cajoles. I feel an agony of guilt building up.* If used in an enclosed space . . . I *know he is staring at me. 'How about you then, Des?' I hear a collective rustle of relief from the rest of the mob now that he has his toe on my throat.* Strike knob sharply on hard surface *. . . I quit. 'Oh, all right then,' I grunt ungraciously. Which is how I came to be on the local RNLI fund-raising committee.*

On the knocker

There is a certain surrealistic quality about collecting for the lifeboat in the deepest heart of rural Suffolk, where roof beams are so low that people lope around at a sort of Quasimodo shuffle. The nearest they get to the surge and roar of salt billows is the Wednesday evening chippy van. I made my way towards a trellissed porch via a wicket gate and daffodils.

'Who is it?' asked an old lady through the letterbox flap.

'It's the lifeboat,' I said absurdly. There should have been a team of snorting horses and men in cork life-preservers but there was just me with my collecting box and floppy tweed hat.

It was a pity about that hat. I had chosen my attire with some care in order to strike a note of respectability but minus opulence. I had on my pachydermic old Gannex mac (*circa* Harold Wilson) and this hat, which was a mistake. With my collar turned up at the back it meant that the brim tipped up and the hat lurched down over my eyes in a sinister fashion. On the other hand, if I crammed it down hard to avoid this effect it splayed out my ears and raised my eyebrows in an expression of frivolous surprise. Defensively I wore my RNLI badge in a prominent position like some holy relic carried by an apprehensive exorcist into a ruined crypt.

The deep strategy that lies behind a local collection is little realised by your cheerful citizen, thudding into lamp-posts as he detours to avoid the pleading eye of the collector. Every district is outlined on the map in felt-tip defining the boundaries which are defended by fencibles with the belligerence of mating robins. Occasionally you may stray into foreign territory.

'They've been round already,' a householder says, implying a visit from some sidling, cold-eyed group carrying violin cases.

The eve-of-collection briefing is short but intense and conducted by the light of guttering candles. Dianne is allotted the council estate, Nigel gets Grudge Street and the sheltered housing and I get a couple of hamlets out in corn-dolly country. A quick hand-clasp, a murmured farewell and we melt into the night with our collecting boxes.

Once you are on the knocker, timing is crucial. At ten in the morning, for instance, the door may be opened by a harassed young mum with a howling baby on one hip and the milk on the cooker about to go critical. She steps back on a smirking cat which erupts with a crackling squawk. Early evenings are best, provided you miss *Dallas*. First, though, comes the dreaded garden path.

'It's the lifeboat,' people hiss from behind curtains. (Nobody has let fly a three-star red.) You've got your cardboard tray round your neck and in it sits your boat-shaped box, a wad of sticky labels, your card of authority, spectacles, pipe and anything else you don't know what to do with. About every fifth gate is a right bastard to undo but occasionally it swings at a touch on well-oiled hinges and your almighty heave sends you plunging in like the start of a bayonet charge. The path seems endless. I have practised an expression of wholesome geniality and a half-smile flickered on and off like a dicky switch. The front door, when you reach it, can be anything from iron-studded black oak to Tesco Georgian and behind it is either Benares brass and agricultural bygones or a bicycle and gumboots where an agricultural bygone answers your knock. 'Thaat's loifboat toime then,' he says with startling insight.

There was a house with a dog. Outside the door was a half-gnawed bone about the size of a human femur. 'Roff, roff, roff,' roared the dog hurling itself at the door with a splintering crash. The door opened, it skidded out, stopped and gave me a highly offensive nudge that brought me up on my tiptoes. 'Hello, lad,' I greeted, giving it a vicious but unseen rap on the muzzle.

Apart from the occasional House of the Dead where the inmates, having seen you coming, crouch silently with spoons half-way to mouths and fingers on the TV mute button, everybody is friendly and generous.

'Would you like to help the lifeboat?' I wheedle to the little old lady. It sounds as if I'm inviting her to lay on to an oar. 'Lifeboat?' I ask another, raising an eyebrow. I shouldn't raise eyebrows I've now decided. Then there was the tall, elderly military gentleman whose erect and soldierly bearing and low door lintel obscured most of his head. 'Lifeboat collectin' ha,' his chin said, 'got to support it ha.' He put three quid's-worth of buoyancy in. Ordinarily you pretend not to look at what they put in, glancing decently aside as though they were adjusting their dentures but this time I bobbed a curtsy.

There is one snag about that tray round the neck. The box had become heavy. I reached for a knocker and it untipped the tray shooting the whole goddam lot on the doormat followed by my floppy tweed hat as I made a grab for it. A surprised housewife opened her door to find a cursing old man scuttling around on hands and knees.

After the house-to-house comes the Saturday grand slam outside the doorway of the local supermarket, which is when you can exploit all the strategems learned on the knocker. You mustn't accost but you can manoeuvre. Tray around neck and badges ready I drifted and glided gracefully to and fro intercepting shoppers as they made for the corners. 'Lifeboat,' I told the sparrows, 'help your lifeboat.'

You can see the mental torture beginning fifty yards away as fingers explore trouser pockets trying to distinguish twenty from five pence coins. I stooped low so that a three-year-old could post coppers with deep breathing concentration, a lengthy ritual and frustrating because the guilty, meanwhile, moving on winged foot, were bolting in left and right like a covey of partridge dodging the guns.

Some were faintly hostile. 'But you already got me at home!' they expostulated, implying a long shot and telescopic sights. You can always pick out the quid donors though – Kangol caps. Always good for a quid is a Kangol cap: headscarves, 30p; anoraks, 10p . . . 'Help your lifeboat.'

When I lived in Essex and sailed from Leigh-on-Sea I was a mud-man – none of your poncing around in white duck trousers and a doeskin jacket. The rig of the day was gumboots, the sort of trousers you'd normally chuck out for a dog's bed and a canvas smock wind-cheater, not that the canvas was ever woven that could cheat the soul-shrivelling Siberian blast of the North Sea. Our boats took the ground on every tide, masts erect one moment then lying at every drunken angle the next, as if a crowd had been swept by a blast of grapeshot. You developed a lurching snowshoe gait for walking on mud, and with the tideline a mile away that was when we'd potter on our drunken boats. The trick was to leave your muddy boots standing alongside and tethered by little painters of codline, otherwise the returning tide caught you unawares. The sight of a row of boots riding in on the flood was the indication that there were beginners about. You learned to judge when to wade ashore, too. A man in thighboots and with an inch of freeboard left made a lovely picture – a ballerina in cloth cap, pipe in mouth, toolbag around neck.

A low run

The equinoxal springs, a term suggesting some bizarre form of gymnastic, produce some sharp tests for the cruising yachtsman.

The extra low run accompanied by big spring tides causes creek beds to give up their grisly secrets like the Day of Judgement while unusual tidal heights transform salting and water meadow into a glittering knee-deep sea, tailor-made to confuse the tyro navigator. Fresh from a winter of adult education – not to be confused with video tapes in plain wrappers and seedy rendezvous above a launderette – the novice with his light dusting of blackboard chalk is eager to practise what he has learned – very little as it happens, due to the twin distractions of an aching buttock and the lecturer's faulty zip.

Heading seaward he searches in vain for the familiar creek boundaries of sedge and supermarket trolley both long since covered, but he sees an avenue of skeletal withies wagging in the current like the admonitory fingers of Earl's Court car park attendants. 'You watch your course and I'll watch the chart,' he admonishes the helmsman testily. It is a division of labour destined to prove meagre in navigational reward but rich in experience. Nobody notices that the withies now sport buds, blossom and in one case a bird-box. A notice warning trespassers of dire retribution flashes past and they judder to a halt on a compost heap.

The mathematically minded student (something big in software) who has mastered the running fix and has a penchant for working out the height of low water to four decimal places finds these tides rich in challenge. Egged on by the pilot book an exploratory zeal grips him, sharpening his susceptibilities and making his eyes water. 'Anchor in utter peace and tranquillity amidst haunts of coot and tern . . .' the book invites coaxingly. He pecks away at his calculator. Having penetrated to the uppermost reaches of the upper reaches and anchored, he sits watching warily the emergence of the seabed – like Moses by the Red Sea, supported by equal measure of faith and computation. 'Cod in cheese or Paella again?' asks Blanche, sorting her boil-in-the-bags. Towering walls of mud rise to port and starboard and crabs stand comfortably in their doorways, looking down on him as if awaiting the passage of a procession; he feels the first twinge of doubt. What he has forgotten in his calculation is British Summertime, a dismal phenomenon at the best of times and of which this is not one. An hour later the grill pan launches itself into space and the boat settles at forty-five degrees. They munch their chocolate digestives amidst the utter tranquillity of popping ooze and on a nightmare croquet court of half-buried motor tyres.

A really low run reveals stinking mysteries merciful-
ly hidden at other times such as the Old Slipway, so-
named by generations of embittered seamen who pro-
ceeded down it whooping seawards on their backs. With
its extremities of gap-toothed planking like a rugby club
piano it is described by the pilot book as '. . . affording
a landing at all states of tide.' It is a description which
could have been applied with more truth to the shell-torn
beaches of the Normandy landings, a helpful note but one
lifted from an earlier, unrevised and out-of-print work by a
long-dead rival. It proves to be scant comfort for the mariner and his lady who land at high tide and return to their
dinghy at low to be faced with a launching akin to tackling
the Cresta Run on a walking frame. He leads while she
pushes the transom, an unwise division of labour. 'Watch
where you place your feet, Nora,' he counsels, stepping
through a gap and vanishing. Her drumming Docksiders

print a pattern of dots across his sun-tanned occiput like some curious parcel franked for posting.

The houseboat owners laid up on the saltings find big spring tides a serious threat to their lifestyle. Long aware of municipal disapproval and Town Hall plans to rate them, they pursue a policy of low profile, a simple enough matter while lying deep in their mud berths and appearing only briefly at high tide like pop-up targets at a funfair, but on the big springs these humble arks are proffered high as if up for auction, revealed in stark detail like bedroom furniture stacked on the garden path by removal men. There is a frantic flattening of cardboard boxes and a shedding of tomato Gro-bags, handle-less perambulators and t.v. aerials. The Borough Surveyor's mate, holding a striped pole, walks backwards with gingerly steps. 'One more pace should do it . . .' says the Surveyor.

To Old Harry the exposed seabed is a trip down memory lane, a route strewn with winch handle, kedge and engine key and where a platoon of vertical teaspoons stand mute witness to the novice washer-up. Backed up in the wire basket of an old fridge the conger eel glowers like some football supporter on the terraces. Here Old Harry is uncrowned king of mooring diggers. No fledgling shoal-water yachtsman can truly claim his heritage until he has buried his own mooring, a sombre-sounding ritual suggesting best navy-blue and a ham tea, but one also rich in traditional expertise.

With the first low run the mooring diggers appear, like some rare spring migrants, oddly plumaged in cloth caps and boilersuits. Shovels over shoulder they tow their sinkers on corrugated iron toboggans, staggering after the retreating ebb as if prospecting along the Yukon trail.

The art is to follow the ebb, judging when to stop and dig so as to allow enough time to boot in the sinker and refill the hole before the flood tide catches them at it. The experts dig with a steady curse-punctuated swing, stacking spoil to form a small circular redoubt, peering out at intervals as if alert for predators. Nearby a novice, heeding no advice, visible only by the flying clods, goes deeper and ever deeper, unaware of his personal impending Niagara. Mooring diggers are like rescue archaeologists flailing away with trowel and teaspoon under the eye of the JCB driver, who sits chin on hand, yawning and glancing at his watch.

Old Harry, doyen of diggers, is ever alert for artefacts of suitable bulk to serve as sinkers, a fact bitterly discovered by the farmer, who thumbs tractor starter-button and is rewarded by the screech betokening a missing flywheel, or the truck driver returning from Joe's Caff to a vehicle perched on a cairn of bricks like some Festival Hall art-form. No sculptor, mallet in hand and gazing at an empty plinth in deep shock, need look further than the bed of Gashouse Creek for the great granite buttocks of his Mother and Child. The chain ferry towed home while making good time towards Ushant bore unmistakable testimony to the sturdy ground tackle chosen to complement this novel sinker.

Perhaps Old Harry's crowning achievement in this field never received full recognition, though. The lady Mayor, her regalia stacked on her mighty bosom like a job lot of teacups at a car boot sale, seized the tasselled cord which operated the curtain concealing the commemorative bronze plaque with a fist like a brick hod. 'And so ay hev great pleasure in opening this new centre,' she trumpeted, tugging lustily. The yawning hole revealed a distant view of Old Harry's converted mussel-drudger riding securely to her new mooring.

71

The sight of a yacht on her ear, the unhappy outcome of a
fluffed calculation or misjudged tack, is common enough in
shoal waters but for a vessel the size of Hoshi *and on a busy*
holiday beach it is spectacular.
Such a sight can be made spectacular even when it's a small
cruiser, if the owner has a penchant for trying out new feats of
seamanship – like heaving-down-by-running-out-the-kedge-
attached-to-the-main-halyard. Which is what I was doing and
under the fascinated gaze of people on other (properly)
anchored yachts nearby.
Now one thing that wives don't take kindly to is being made the
target for curious eyes and Joyce is no exception. I had the
kedge laid well off, halyard bent to it and I was sweating and
grunting on the halyard winch with the boat already steeply
heeled, everything humming and more binoculars trained on
us than Beecher's Brook.
'What . . . I . . . want you to . . . do' I gasped through clenched
teeth, heaving, 'is . . . go forward and . . . heave on the . . .
main . . . anchor.' Joyce stood firm. 'Right,' she said. 'Now I'll
tell you what I will do. If you don't stop these ridiculous antics
at once, I shall row straight ashore in the dinghy!'

A horse and cart astern

There comes a moment when you can see it all going
horribly wrong. The whole operation has the mark of the
beast upon it and yet nobody does anything about it. There
you all stand, like wet hens under a barrow, listening to the
engine note, watching the dip and swing of the bows and
noting the inch-a-minute crawl of foam alongside.

It was just such a situation. Astern lay the open
gates of the lock and we could have scuttled back in
again before they closed, but we didn't; we all stood there

heeling-and-toeing as she pitched into the dead noser that had confronted us from the moment we had left the lock. The channel, flanked by shallows and a training wall on one side, led straight out over the drying sands, seaward, and our ageing, snuffling, feeble auxiliary just nudged us over the ground at a crawl. The helmsman gripped his spokes and wore an expression of costive disapproval; I was the helmsman.

The lock gates closed behind us. Half a mile to go before we could set some sail and pay off on a safe slant. We pitched, screwed, paused, pitched again and paused again. A dead crab alongside seemed set to beat us to the post. Nobody spoke. Nobody mentioned what we were all thinking; that if the engine stopped we would have a panic on our hands. To have mentioned the fact would have been like using the word 'funereal' in the house of the lately bereaved.

We could anchor, I thought. Then, no we couldn't anchor because we'd be set athwart by the now appreciable beam tidal current. Then what the hell *could* we do?

'God it's stopped,' everybody said, unnecessarily and together. 'It's bloody *stopped*,' the skipper confirmed, making it official. God received the news unmoved. The spell was broken by the jerking and jangling of gear aloft and the lip-smacking water beneath the counter. The wheel died on me and I waited for orders.

'Get the mainsail and jib on her.'

The schooner mainsail had a standing gaff, brailed like barge and it was set within seconds. The jib did its usual belly wobble, being set flying; it filled and I let her head off to port as ordered and steadied on full-and-bye. We hung there chopping at it, like an old horse with bad teeth chomping turnips.

'Foresail.'

The gaff foresail baggy-trousered its way up the old schooner's foremast, shook, rattled and filled. We began to heel promisingly and the wheel came alive in my hands but something was wrong. We were heeling and heaving, the sound effects were OK too but we were like a pirate ship in pantomime, heaving around and getting nowhere; all I lacked was an eye-patch and a cardboard parrot. Ho, ho, bloody ho.

The new heading was taking us out over the shallow flats. There were no echo sounders in those days and nobody took a sounding, perhaps because we all knew that whatever depth we got, it wouldn't be enough. It *felt* shallow. The soles of our shoes told us so. It was like treading on untried ice. Then I understood what was happening; we were 'smelling bottom' as the old lads used to say, with such stark poetry. As the old ship tried to pick up speed the disturbance she created swept the seabed a few feet below her and created drag.

'We'll put her about as soon as we have way enough,' said the skipper. We could have bacon and eggs, if we had the bacon – and the eggs. So we stood on, waiting, hoping, wincing. Then we tried it. Helm down and up she came, clipped a crest off, shook, hung, fell astern and paid off back on her old course.

Somebody was trying the engine for the umpteenth time and the starter motor had reached that weary flat-battery stage, wow-pause-wow-longer pause-wow. Then we hit.

Let's not go mad describing it. If it has ever happened

to you, you'll know and if it hasn't then you'll just have to wait until it does. It will, some day.

We had all sagged at the knee and called in ragged chorus upon our Maker in terms ranging from rank blasphemy to devout hope. The long masts wagged as she hit again and something in the galley fell with a clatter. She heeled to a puff, strode forward again and hit a third time.

If we had anchored there and then we would at least have stood a chance on the next tide, being well out on the seaward edge of the flats, but of course we didn't. We all went square-jawed and resolute, which is about as helpful as trying to argue around an expired season ticket. As the tide fell, our crashes became first more regular, then continuous and then with the keel firmly on we began to heel and take it on the port bilge.

A stoutly-built long-keeled hull pounding on her keel is one thing; it is like landing flat on your feet with the whole framework of your body absorbing the shock. Pounding on her bilge is something else; then, you are landing on your hip bone which is both bloody painful and fraught with danger. So we hammered and pounded for an hour or more, spars whipping and everything sliding. I felt sick to my guts. I loved that old lady and every blow was personal.

And then, at last we were dry. The last trickle of water left her and she lay at an absurd angle, masts pointing shorewards to the bathing beach and the confetti of distant holidaymakers. French holidaymakers.

First on the scene was an old man in a beret, riding a bicycle and smoking a fag. He rode right round us, nodded *bonjour* as if the encounter was of a normality that required no further display of emotion, and headed back shorewards.

They came in droves. Sultry girls all belly button and suntan, chin-fringed young men, well-equipped matrons in swimming suits with hip fringes, designed to disguise and achieving the effect of delicatessen hams, middle-aged men with curious ankles and children by the plague. With them came the horse and cart.

It drove right round us.

Right the way round us with the driver pointing out hull features of especial interest to his passenger. It was like having someone peep up your kilt. We suffered it in stony British silence, upper lips so stiff that we spoke like ventriloquists' dolls.

A gingerish dog scouted around busily in the area of our cutwater and, inspired, cocked its leg. Slowly the crowd dispersed. There was just one anxious mother remaining and she had by the hand a small and thoughtful-looking infant. There, under the protective curve of our run she dropped its drawers.

'That's just about bloody done it,' somebody said.

And how did it all end? Our charter party left us, skipper and me. Our insurance company, finding us nicely neaped and without future ordered an ocean-going tug from Le Havre. A keel trench was dug seawards, cable laid out and buoyed, hull girdled to take the strain and in due course we were dragged off half afloat, with the rudder rammed up into the trunking and the wheel standing up on end like a daisy. We had a month in Le Havre being repaired and living off the proceeds of the empty wine bottles (which were accepted back in those days) left by our lotus-eating charterers. They had wined well.

Eventually, since we couldn't afford to get paid help, we flogged her back across Channel, dead noser. We were worn out. When that mooring buoy came aboard I fondled it like Hamlet with his skull. Skipper said, absently, 'I've never liked horses.'

I've never owned a fast boat. I can be overtaken and feel not the slightest stir of competitive unease. There was a period when we joined in the club cruiser handicap races, which almost put our marriage in jeopardy due to my radical racing tactics and the embarrassment of ending up at the head of the fleet as it caught us up on the second round.
I've tried reading books about making boats go faster (plain wrappers) which advised me to ease my luff, flatten my Cunningham, buff my bottom and adjust my slot but the speedo needle continues to struggle feebly at the bottom of the scale like some insect blasted with DDT. Our boats tend to be powerful, comfortable in a seaway, directionally stable and excellent sea-keepers. But then so are the lighthouses.

With a bone in her teeth

The advent of the marine speedometer has spelt curtains to the social gaiety of the cockpit. Where once the helmsman held laughing court with his audience spellbound at the sparkling rhetoric, bleak silence now reigns. No schoolboy carpenter notes the application of setsquare to his grinning mortise joint with more foreboding than does the helmsman eyeing that tell-tale clock.

'I think the wind must have taken off a shade,' hazards our Percy, trying to account for the flagging needle, 'I had her up to ten a moment ago.' The owner, who knows that you couldn't get her up to ten knots even on a hand-cart down a cliff face treats this claim with naked disbelief and takes up a stance abaft the wheel. Percy's ears light up like lift buttons and he begins fisting the spokes as if he were juggling with dumb-bells.

The comforting knowledge that no boat can be shoved along faster than her maximum designed speed under sail provides blessed relief for many a half-hearted owner being pressed, half-heartedly, by his crew to set the spinnaker.

'Well I'm as keen as the next man,' he states accurately, 'and I'd say "yes" in a flash if it would help.' They all sigh with relief, boom out the genoa and congratulate each other on a wise and seamanlike decision.

Old Harry, comfortable in the theory that the more you stick up the faster you go, reaches his designed maximum four and a half knots under jumbo and bonnet, thereafter rolling up the sea ahead of him like a piano on a rag rug. 'Let's see if we can put a bone in her teeth,' he offers, setting a jackyard topsail, a Jimmy Green and a reeking marquee of mildewed cotton. Immediately a great hole yawns under her counter into which she squats like a punctured ball-cock.

The art of enjoying a slow boat is never to sail in company with a faster one. Witness the little family cruiser with a midship section like a tin chapel. 'Look, she's going like a train,' chants the delighted owner innocent of an ironical reference to her fitful and laboured progress. The

rub comes when a strange sail heaves in sight. Elated to the point of belligerence he gives chase at once. A short while later, gazing stiffly away from her receding transom, he begins to feel like last man in the father's day sack race. 'Those things are all right if you don't mind discomfort,' he jeers, darting a look of newly-awakened disgust at his own lofty coachroof.

The speedometer, reading as optimistically as a holiday camp brochure, has brought sail trimming to a pitch of refinement which leaves no time for the helmsman's mate to brood down the open hatch at the little cameo of luxury below. Simulating keenness at half-hourly intervals for the benefit of any top brass listening below, he gives the sheet winch a couple of pawls, cries out in triumph, then promptly checks them back again – a little deception condoned by the yawning helmsman.

The true enthusiast is the real menace. An encouraging response from the needle fires him to trim out the last vestige of weather helm. The traditionalist, raised in an age when weather helm was thought as essential to windward work as sulphur and treacle to establishing healthy thoughts in the minds of the young, is left feeling as if he were steering a tiny tot's fire engine on a funfair roundabout. He begins making a course like an Ouija board message.

Relief comes only with the fouling of transducer or pitot ('I think his pitot is foul'). The needle plunges dramatically to zero and racing owners stare in numb disbelief, like the purchaser of a postal bargain duffle coat watching it come through the letter box.

The dinghy man, his pants skimming the water in a 10-knot plane, regards speed as his personal prerogative and bitterly resents its display by any other craft. The runabout owner, hounded out to sea by a dripping Harbourmaster and waved farewell by the inverted and pedalling feet of pram dinghy oarsmen, is as popular with dinghy sailors as a scratching dog under a tea trolley.

'Places changed rapidly,' scribble yachting correspondents as the curling wake wreaks havoc among the leaders and diapered trapeze crews hover on beating pinions. It takes the arrival of Old Harry with a following wind and a jammed halyard to restore good humour and order. With his sucking wake already tenanted by a pedalo, a selection of beach balls and a sunbather on a Li-Lo, lucky are the helmsmen who can manoeuvre within reach of its foaming orbit.

I was once put in command of a working party of old sweats. It was my first command as a lance corporal in a transit camp peopled by all the hop-heads and chuck-outs rejected by a score of battalions. It was an exhibition of military might to strike fear at the heart of the enemy. A load of cookhouse coke had been dumped outside the fuel compound gates and it was my job to see that it was shovelled inside, perhaps not a task which called for much in the way of tactical brilliance but I blew it just the same. I made three serious errors: to begin with I never thought to take a list of names, secondly I elected to march at the head of my force instead of bringing up the rear, and thirdly I used my initiative. Thus, I arrived at the coalyard gate and called out the command to halt with only one weedy youth remaining, the rest having scarpered at every bend and corner along the route. There was a civilian contractor's bulldozer working nearby. 'Would five bob see that coke shoved inside during the dinner hour?' I asked the driver. 'I reckon it might, squire,' he said, pocketing it. The youth and I repaired to the NAAFI for tea, wads and bread pudding slabs. When we returned to the yard the coke was all inside – so were both gates and a few yards of fence.

So long at the fare

I had always been a champion of good country fare. Show me a home-made apple tart and even though the air was filled with the ricochet and whine of fragmentation when I put fork to pastry I would wag an appreciative head and stack it away. Shop cake would have me backed up in a corner wearing an old-time Basil Rathbone sneer, I would have no truck with your factory jam and my comment on the sliced loaf was a coarse laugh of disgust. All that was before I met farmhouse brawn.

In foreign lands I have met with sausages that were active enough to wear a county cap and I have seen meat loaves charged with static and vibrating steadily on the slab which would have had about the same effect on your digestion as a clock weight, but compared with that brawn they are so much dear dolly mixture.

It was when I was a lance corporal of three days' standing that I met farmhouse brawn. Command weighed heavily upon me at the time. We were on a scheme in the Yorkshire Dales. I had a patrol and my men did exactly as I told them. I told them to take cover on a bracken-covered hillside. Later, when I tried to rally them I was faced with a mile of bracken which reverberated with contented snores and a pall of cigarette smoke that was bringing down a wasp's nest of bicycling umpires.

I was back-tracking along the valley when I found the farmhouse. I was a figure to inspire terror in mid-calf denim trousers and the tin hat with the single wilting frond of bracken, and as I ran my gaiters were shuttling up and down my ankles like serviette rings on a couple of whet-stones. The farmer, though, had nothing but compassion written large on his patriarchal features. 'I'm just puttin' 't kittle on. How about a sup and a bite son,' he said. I skidded to a halt.

I was expecting the old home-cured ham and the old gooseberry tart with clotted war-effort cream. I was inside that door so fast that I drove my tin hat down over my ears with a brisk click like a pickle jar lid. When I had prised it up again a strange sight met my eyes.

The farmer had placed a plate upon the table. On the plate a grey object nodded at me. I smiled and prodded it with my finger. 'Very good,' I said. 'Very life-like especially about the eyes.'

'I'll be back in a minute lad,' he said, 'tuck in now, an' don't be afraid of it.' He left me standing there with my smile slipping down around my neck like a horse collar. That brawn – for as such I had identified it by then – looked like some rare culture magnified through a microscope. There were more tubes in it than a map of the Metro, great rocks of gristle studded it like some nightmare Bonanza, it shuddered and shook at some maniacal joke of its own. A medical student would have been spellbound.

I am no fool in an emergency. I had it whipped off that plate in my fist and was making for the fireplace before you could have said 'trachenchyma'. Unhappily I found that the fireplace was boarded up and guarded by a stuffed heron. It had a discouraged expression and held

a papier maché fish in its beak, it was apparently in the same fix as I was. I got back to the table and slapped that brawn back on my plate a split second before the farmer reappeared. He asked how it was going. I told him I just couldn't put it away fast enough. He disappeared again to feed his fowls.

This time I made for the window. It hadn't been opened since Cromwell but I had it up in one heave. When the cloud of dead flies and beetle dust had cleared, there was my benefactor coming around the corner.

'Ha ha. I see you,' I babbled insanely. I closed the window and tidied the cobwebs back in place. A moment later he was at my side loaded with suspicion. When he saw my clean and shining plate though, he beamed. 'Well, you certainly got that acrost your chest lad,' he congratulated me warmly. I faced him bowing a little from the waist in a manner reminiscent of a more courtly age and thanked him for his hospitality. I was still bowing from the waist as I stepped outside and into the arms of my platoon commander. He went up like a rocket. His address was delivered at some length and covered a variety of aspects concerning my suitability for command . . . 'and get your shoulders back man,' he advised, touching the upper register, *get your shoulders back!'*

I got them back. The soggy, tremulous *bomb of brawn* moulded itself lovingly to my sternum and began to melt.

The application of antifouling paint to deter the growth of weed, barnacle and other living jewels of the depths is one of the penalties of ownership, also of the paint manufacturers who try to come up with compounds fatal to encrustations but which can be applied safely by flap-eared, drivelling cretins without poisoning themselves.
Painting a boat's bottom ranks with eighteenth-century child labour in terms of human misery. You kneel, crouch, roll on your back, hump, twist and gyrate on wet concrete and in a biting wind while the foul stuff dribbles up your arm, up your trouser leg and behind both ears – two coats of it. You can try a paint roller of course but then the dog stands in the paint tray and prints its route up the ladder and right along the coachroof, as if marking out a nature trail.

What's that on your bottom?

That the yachtsman now ranks in the eyes of conservationists as a poisoner of the under-sea environment, a vandal, aerosol in hand, about to do over a phone box, is a bitter pill for those of us who hoard our gash like some valuable family heirloom. Every scrap is examined closely to assess its biodegradability before giving it the deep six. On the sea-bed a hermit crab studies an eggshell critically before trying it on for size; it resolves to do something about its hip measurement.

The culprit is our antifouling paint. Father, still in deep shock after learning its price per litre, which would make spreading it thinly on French toast more fitting than sloshing it on a hull, has to work under the scowling regard of protestors with Save our Barnacle banners. He appears at the top of the ladder. 'I've just been castigated,' he raves shrilly. Not that the annual ceremony of antifouling is a festival of fun at the best of times.

The day chosen brings an Arctic wind which has met little on its way from Bear Island before reaching the bare inch of flesh between vest and pants. As the first tin is opened a thin drizzle sets in and, while mum is trying to spread hard butter on soft rolls with a penknife, father below, with his purple wattles drooping like a knitted bathing suit, slaps away in joyless silence.

Having started off by reading the warnings on the tin and being conscious of cost, he lays on the first strokes with the narrowed eye and steady hand of the miniaturist busy on locket and snuff-box. At intervals a dribble of water emerges from a cockpit drain with the regularity of a municipal toilet flush; a spider peers out from the log impeller with more curiosity than wisdom. By the time half the second coat is on, he is laying about him like a Crusader defending Jerusalem. Mother, long since wearied of his sighing patience at her ineptitude with the brush (it is small, solid and sporting a vestigial scut of usable bristle), has climbed aboard to rinse the mugs. 'Oh, what would I give for a small wetted surface,' father mourns, shifting to stand exactly under the galley sink drain.

For the full measure of drama, though, the job should be started in boots, on tiptoe as the tide ebbs and completed like an exam paper in mindless frenzy on the returning flood. 'What I'd really like is a wet suit,' he notes, stepping back and falling over the dog. The alternative is roller painting, an art mastered by Old Harry and aided by a huge roller the manufacture of which coincided with the disappearance of a rolling pin and a neighbourhood cat. Nearby owners give him a wide berth and watch from concealment.

While the application of masking tape to the waterline in half freezing gale may leave a few marital wounds to be healed and produce a line like a seismic trace of Krakatoa, it is the unfortunate coincidence that the only suitable antifouling day should clash with the Bensons' cocktail party in the evening that really slaps the boot in the custard.

'How often do I get the chance to dress up and look nice; go on just tell me,' she challenges. 'I can't go on.

I'm finished, *finished* do you hear,' she wails. Helpfully he points out a patch on the other side of the rudder which belies this statement.

They will not be the only folk at the party to be sporting the spring plumage of the yachtsman: Band-Aid pennants cracking bravely in the breeze and patches of Copolymer and Trawler Red on ear lobe and elbow lending a touch of heraldry to the festive scene. It doesn't matter how long you sit in the cooling swamp of the bathtub grinding away with the pumice; there are always patches that are missed, to be eyed by fellow guests with sidelong compassion.

'Look, I see she's had her ends tinted,' hisses a woman wearing what appears to be a black Bedouin tent. 'Personally I'd rather let it go grey all over.' At the County Court a learned judge consults a wristwatch with a strap speckled red like some outlandish jungle egg. The parson in his church raises benedictory fingers of mottled blue. The doctor in his surgery eyes the brilliant Meccano kneecaps of his patient with scorn. 'You'll need at least two scrubs by September,' he prophesies discouragingly.

With a smart breeze down the river many a vessel will heel to reveal a luxuriant row of patches along her bilge – a legacy of yard byelaws forbidding owners to shift their own hull shores, but Old Harry laughs to scorn such strictures. 'The starboard one's got her,' he explains, knocking out the remaining port one. Ethel's boy Sidney trots into view carrying a shore. He watches the dust cloud of Old Harry's retreat with the slowly dawning comprehension of some scholar deciphering a clay tablet.

Contemptuous of trade products, Old Harry uses a private and secret formula handed down from father to son, with shifty relief by the former and the wary acceptance of a ticking bomb by the latter. It is fatal to windsurfers at fifty yards. The recipe for this poisonous nostrum would make the dread secret of Glamis Castle sound like a tip for discouraging greenfly. Applied hot with a brush that would win prizes in a dahlia show and just prior to launching, the water boils and burps briefly as the vessel descends the slip, foreshore crabs leg it up the beach and a nearby angler's bait choosing the better of two depressing alternatives begins shinning back up the line in panic. There is an area of sea-bed downtide of his mooring that looks like the morning after Crecy. Half a mile downstream and standing waist deep, a healthy old gentleman (high fibre and low church) prepares for his morning plunge. 'By God this is the stuff,' he diagnoses with unwitting accuracy. 'This'll set me up for the day!' A distant expression creeps over his face. He gives a falsetto whoop and leaves the water like a Trident missile.

Fortunately for the environment this fearful paint is of short-term efficacy and by mid-season Old Harry's underwater surfaces look like an old English sheepdog, a succulent wonderland of marine growth where barnacles bursting with rude health jostle for space with athletic gribble and grinning mussel. A paint chemist sitting on his test raft watches enviously as this dripping, popping feast goes by. At haul-out time, learned professors of marine biology gather to watch with rapture as the trolley trundles and the spitting mass heaves into view; mussels snap shut with the finality of a club barman slamming the shutters down.

Old Harry is not usually given to acts of physical violence as he later explained in the Magistrate's Court; neither was he to know that the venerable old don who was hurrying forward eagerly uncorking his specimen bottle was dually afflicted by a cleft palate and a squint. At the time, Old Harry was bending massively to inspect the growth. 'Just look at them,' mumbled the scholar indistinctly and gazing in a peculiar direction. 'You've got the biggest polyps I've ever seen!'

The skipper of a makee-learnee yacht ploughs a stony furrow,
beset as he is on the one hand by the multiple perils of the deep
and on the other by the ineptitudes of the earnest but bumbling
efforts of the landsman.
On deck and eager to lend a hand they come rocking after you
in their huge new gymshoes to stand immediately behind you
as you heave, haul and grunt. You step backwards with deep
and secret satisfaction on yielding toes. 'Oh sorry,' you cry,
side-swiping somebody with a winch handle. 'Hope I didn't
hurt you,' you mourn falsely, butting somebody in the groin.
They are indefatigable and indestructible.
You reach shelter after a long and harrowing night, haggard,
bog-eyed and utterly weary. The anchor goes down. 'Aren't
you going to exhibit your black ball?' askes a neophyte,
blinking rapidly. There is no fair reply to this so you clench
your teeth and shudder. I once went off watch totally bushed.
'Call me if anything worries you,' I told the mate of the watch.
He called me just as my soul was quitting its earthly envelope.
'Skipper, skipper!' I reared up as if I'd heard the Last Trump,
'Yes, yes, what's wrong?' He leaned forward confidentially.
'There's something nasty blocking the toilet.'

Up the peak

It was the early fifties. The firey ovens of war had cooled
leaving a peace – a soufflé that had gone flat. Stunned
by anti-climax, people needed some new excitement and
many turned to the sea, which was how the Island Cruising Club was born. This unique boat-owning co-operative
was started on a shoestring with two big old vessels, a malodorous mountain of blankets and skeleton staff (dietary
deficiency) who fitted out by end-for-ending everything
on the first Sunday in Lent. Our ripe and blotchy sails

90

looked like the Bayeux Tapestry and even our baggy-wrinkle had dandruff, but we knew we could get away with murder provided it was done in a proper seamanlike manner.

Our members were a cross-section of the populace, but like farmhouse brawn it didn't pay to peer too closely at it. Now and again we'd get an ex-sailor who could fire an oerlikon gun – a talent of limited value aboard a seventy foot gaff schooner – but for the most part everybody came to us in a state of nautical virginity. My wife was mate/cook and I was the skipper. The only reason we hoisted a burgee was to keep the vultures from roosting on the main truck.

Saturday was turn-round day, when we got rid of one lot and squared up ready for the next. Down they'd come on the 4.10P.M. bus from Kingsbridge in their Hepworth caps and cycle capes. They would take one long look down the harbour at the undulations of Salcombe bar and swallow hard in quick succession, their Adam's apples shuttling up and down like ping-pong balls in a shooting gallery. Meanwhile, out on the mooring, Joyce and I would be distributing the sheet-bags. Since it is likely that these exercised a powerful influence on the uninformed maritime mind, they deserve special mention. Designed with an eye to economy they were stout enough to take a couple of roundshot at the feet should occasion warrant and all were of the same length – short. According to your build you got either a winding sheet or a nocturnal sack race. And they were narrow. All it took was a few revolutions in your bunk plus a handful of rare oils and unguents and you were wrapped up and ready for the Valley of the Kings.

'Here they come,' Joyce would warn. We would rig smiles as the club launch, with about as much freeboard as a lily pad, lurched alongside. Our quota was usually ten souls with us sleeping down the sail locker, making a crew of twelve, although on occasion we made it fourteen. Working ship was like army netball.

They were not all males. We'd get a few lady librarians with an attack of the Masefields, thin girls in search of

Truth, fat ones avoiding it, healthy jolly girls clad in rug wool and a great many nurses. We liked nurses. Take Judy Russell who, in the course of time, succeeded me as skipper of *Hoshi*. Nurses can handle men. All men are awed by their own bowels (Rodin's famous statue The Thinker wasn't waiting for a bus), and aware of the awful powers of persuasion invested in the nursing profession. Judy in her wrath was a Boadicea of the Bedpan and could inject her commands with a note of bleakness that would subdue the haughtiest of males. 'We haven't sweated up our peak today have we?' she would rasp.

Once we had shown people where they were going to sleep and they had believed it, they would change into their Milletts War Surplus sailing gear and start wandering forlornly around the deck, the men in vast pairs of shorts like torpedo tubes from which, in lieu of those deadly missiles, there protruded legs of a celery whiteness terminating in speckled sandshoes hugely new. Flapping and squeaking they would parade up and down as though impelled by clockwork. From down below it sounded like the applause for a chapel concert conjurer.

Then would come The First Supper.

Sometimes there would be an eve-of-battle camaraderie about it, a rakehellish gustiness through which there stalked the sly spectre of foreboding for the morrow, but on other occasions all you would hear would be the pecking of forks and the occasional ricochet as a split pea hit the deckhead. It would then be my job to break the ice.

We could get ten people round the saloon table with me sitting on the cold bogey stove at the head, but only if they sat sideways. It was like addressing a stack of pennies, a double row of silently munching profiles, and trying to keep the merry ball of wit and conversation in flight was like playing squash with a beanbag. I had one topic though that never failed to start everybody talking at once. Dental treatment. Everybody had a gruelling tale to tell and raconteurs of chair and drill would shout each other down while I sat and relaxed. Until one night . . .

He had not joined in. He was a little man whose back hair stood up shocked as though by the sight of some permanent and personal ghoul. While being bald in front, his head created the clever illusion of a small airship stuck in the hangar door. The yarns were coming thick and fast as old memories flooded back. 'Why I remember one tricky filling I had,' somebody was saying. The airship cleared its throat. '*I'm a dentist,*' he said. There was total silence. There was a bread-and-butter pudding to follow. It was like watching boa-constrictors tackling goats.

Sunday morning meant sail drill, which is the whole point of this damn story if I ever get to it. I'd have them all up on deck and I'd warn them about wasting water, blocking the heads, saving lights and how to be seasick while keeping a stiff upper lip in a proper British manner (no pretty sight); also how to set and handle the sails. An old lady watching from the shore had once commended me warmly. 'I often watch you holding Sunday morning service,' she'd said.

A gaff schooner may have some thirty to forty bits of running gear in more or less regular use. A new green crew standing back to back, arms dangling, gazes upwards at the swaying, thwacking thickets of sisal like a package tour party in the Tomb of Napoleon. A long

morning looms ahead. Seizing a hand at random, I prise open the fingers and wrap them around a rope. 'Tops'l tack tackle fall,' I enunciate clearly and meaninglessly. 'Tickle Topsy's Tail?' repeats the tyro hopefully.

Or you can do it the other way, teaching from scratch about the drifting leaf on the woodland pool, the soaring flight of the gull (on edge), working onwards via lateral resistance to the Reynold's Factor and coffee and biscuits in numbed silence. How to haul, coil, sweat up and belay comes as light relief, but with thirty foot of solid pitchpine as a main boom and no winches it is all hands to the mainsheet when 'Gybe-O' comes the merry cry and the winds are piping strong. Gybing was my personal nightmare.

'All I want to impress upon you and *beg* of you is that when you hear me shout *come up* you just *let go*,' I would plead, studying each face in turn with emotion, wondering which of them would do it on me that trip. 'Just open the hands by straightening out the fingers so that I can get enough slack to take a turn.' They'd stare back at me nodding complete comprehension. A dummy run would be called for. They would line up along the sheet.

'To-me Aggh, to-me Ug, to-me Wahey,' I'd chant, hauling slack sheet through the blocks while, tailed on behind, my team would bump and shunt like trucks in a siding.

'To-me *hah, come up behind!*' They would drop the sheet as if it was connected to the National Grid while I strove to snatch a turn on the bitts. All except one. There is always, always one of them who hangs on and at sea the mainsheet runs smoking and sizzling across your shins as you muff your turns.

On this occasion though there was the one vital difference that Sunday morning. Our new crew included The Man Who Had Been Before. Now this could be a very good thing but it depended upon how long since. A year is a long time and recollections gather substance. During this time a chap dines out on the yarn about how he alone muzzled the flogging jib, forgetting the skylight he stuck his boot through and the buckets he lost. When he disembarked the year before he was still in a state of mild shock. Limping ashore with a shackle pin in one shoe he had staggered up the hill sobbing his mother's name. He returns a year later with a rolling gait, a knife on a lanyard and fancy sennit from glottis to Y-fronts.

Norman was his name, a fellow Yorkshireman wearing a flat cap and braces; he had a suggestion. 'Give everybody a few ropes at a time does't see?' he explained, 'then 'appen we can *orchestrate* 'em.' I'd been aware of the mutterings on the mess deck. You've lobbied them you bastard, I thought. The man who could orchestrate that lot could plait worms. On the other hand if I didn't give them the chance to discover the snivelling futility of the crazy idea, why then the first cock-up that occurred at sea would be laid at my door. I could just imagine the little sneers and the shrugs as the tail of the throat halyard rattled aloft and the jib fell by the run. Orchestrate them. I looked at my trombone section in its towering woolly bobble caps and my woodwinds in their vast khaki shorts and I shuddered. 'Well, we might try it,' I said cravenly.

I left him to it and went below so that I could snoop through the saloon skylight. At first there was the mainsail performing the usual drunken jerks and staggers like a fat old camel struggling to its feet and the gaff foresail tiredly rising and falling; the foreboom rose mysteriously and fell with a crash. Time passed. I got interested in an old *Woman's Own*. Then Norman stuck his head down the companionway. 'Would you like to come an' have a look at this?' he invited with the suppressed excitement of one surgeon nudging a colleague. I went up on deck.

As if he had rapped his baton suddenly, those sails were rising and falling in rhythmic succession like the wings of a homing heron. The anticipatory sneer faded from my lips to be replaced by the bitter moue of grudging awe. 'All the same,' I told a girl with a figure like a deckchair in a sack, 'I'd like to see a few more wrinkles round your nock'; and to a youth with an embryo moustache and patterned socks who was on the staysail, 'you've got a couple of hanks undone.' He grabbed guiltily at his buttons.

Sailing time that day was 1400 on the first lick of ebb, which was important as we didn't rate our engine too seriously. We *had* one but like the garden swing seat up in the garage rafters its value was disproportionate to the hassle of bringing it into play and keeping it going. On the way down harbour I preferred to be at the wheel rather than kneeling at the foot of the companionway with my ear cocked.

With a fair wind and tide we lay bows up-river which meant a 180 degree swing to turn her. We put the jib in stops and a backspring on the buoy. 'Up mainsail,' I ordered. Hands sprang to allotted tasks each in frowning concentration as Norman conducted his little symphony of movement. The mainsail rose silkily, gaff perfectly horizontal in the proper manner, then a pause as the throat purchase clicked and rendered and up went the peak until the requisite wrinkles appeared at the throat; it was movingly lovely.

'Jib,' I said in a hushed voice, afraid of defiling this holy moment. The breaking stops snapped and fluttered down as the starboard sheet came home and the jib aback spread its blotches and patches to the breeze. I put on a few spokes of port wheel and she began to sheer. 'Let go forward.' She dropped aft against the backspring and began turning faster and faster downwind, her bowsprit cutting an arc against the distant shore. 'Let slip spring,' I told Joyce, for I trusted no other at that job at that stage. A backspring to a mooring buoy is as reliable a source of fun for onlookers as the entry of Widow Twanky. Then we were round and heading down harbour for the open sea heeling a little, bow wave chuckling. It knew something.

'Nice work everybody,' I congratulated, 'now let's see what you can do with the foresail?' Which was tantamount to watching a comic weighing a custard pie in one hand and asking if you could have some.

We must have made a brave sight outward bound that day for goodness knew what salty adventures, with boats griped in for sea and colours fluttering. Ashore full many a throat swallowed its lump. 'Foresail then if you please,' I said with a touch of the Hornblowers. There was a bustle of activity around the foot of the foremast as each specialist ran to his or her own cleat or pin. Off came the gaskets. There was a clicking of patent blocks and the throat of the sail shot up the mast. The peak of the gaff didn't move, it stayed where it was hanging limply vertical. 'Peak, peak,' I called, 'come on peak halyard!' The sail now looked like a poorly pitched bell-tent. 'Oh *belay that*,' I shrilled. 'No don't make it fast,' I begged as the throat halyard man, satisfied with the accomplishment of his personal best, began packing successive figures-of-eight on the pin. 'Look, lower the bloody thing!' I howled reverting to the twentieth century.

'Norman,' I said, pitching my voice to a calm and reasonable note, 'they simply must keep that gaff horizontal, throat and peak hauling together like the mainsail.'

'Oh aye, I knaw that, but . . .' began Norman.

'Now,' I said gently, breathing strongly through my nostrils, 'up foresail.'

Exactly the same thing happened again. 'Down, down, down,' I begged. Down it came at a run. What unmanned me more than this pitiful spectacle though was that nobody seemed *worried*. Every face wore the same expression of patient self-satisfaction, all awaiting my next idiotic command.

'If we could wait a couple o' minutes,' Norman said, winking conspiratorially.

'No we bloody can't. I want that sail up *now*. Go and see what the hell your peak halyard chap is up to.'

'Ah but that's just it.'

'What's just it?'

Norman brought his lips close to my ear, a soul of tact with a little secret to share. 'The peak halyard's in't toilet,' he whispered confidentially.

Note: It really did happen. What may be a little further from the truth is that my portrayal of that greenhorn crew as a howling bunch of ten-thumbed cretins is not strictly accurate. It might well have been the next lot. It was thirty years ago.

Extra note: Nowadays the Island Cruising Club is a paragon of efficiency with a fleet of yachts maintained in prime condition and members wear very brief shorts indeed.

And a 'nock', as everybody knows, is the fore upper corner of a gaff mainsail. I was asked to write a short survey of the yachting fraternity by the Sunday Observer and the more I thought about it the lousier the idea seemed. Yachting folk carry their dread secret as if they were members of some outlawed occult society, alert for the private signals that identify a fellow believer. 'What have you got on your bottom this year?' they hiss over a cocktail glass, or 'Get her across this summer?' The reply is equally potent with meaning: 'She doesn't like beating. I couldn't get many good fixes either.' The early Christians, nipping in and out of the catacombs like pop-up targets, knew the same sort of censure and maintained the same sort of tight-lipped low profile. The ordinary decent folk you find behind any Tesco-Georgian front door don't tolerate 'that sort of thing' and 'what yachtsmen do in private is their own affair,' they say dramatically, 'so long as they don't flaunt it in public.'

The agony of a wrinkled nock

The typical yachtsman with horizon-searching eyes and strong white teeth gripping friendly briar only exists in the tobacco advertisements. He can be small, pale and shifty, long-haired or wearing a shirt like the back bedroom wallpaper. You cannot pick him out in a crowd until he opens his mouth; then the crowd edges away a bit. 'I gave her a good bash on Sunday,' he tells an uneasy neighbour, 'right round the Buxey. Flogged her up the Swin on short legs, and then had it free all the way home.'

Yachtsmen lurk in railway compartments. You have your usual bunch – flat caps and flannels, shopping bags, art silk bloomers, clawing infants – and this yachtsman disguised in flat cap and flannels.

Picking out a yachtsman

The system works in reverse. You could stand up in church and yell, 'Gybe O!' Half a dozen dinghy sailors would duck, the parson would grab his lectern and the

organist, a cruising man, would blow two hoots and turn to port. Yachting gets in the blood. You can pick out a yachtsman in the springtime by his blue, green, Bitumastic or red lead fingernails, or on Monday mornings in the summer, in the City, by his concertina collar and muddy socks. On Friday afternoons he has ten fathoms of inch-and-a-half pre-stretched Terylene rope bulging his briefcase and he is catching a train at 3.30 P.M.

Once afloat, yachtsmen revert to type, splitting into factions as remote from each other as opening day at Crufts. They unite to rescue each other, clap at club dinners, and curse outboard runabouts, but they are otherwise divided.

There is the racing keel-boat man walking two inches above the ground and looking exactly like what a yachtsman should look exactly like. You have your old-school motor yachtsman, juggling flags at sunset in a bumper yachting cap like a successful souffle, and then there is your Royal Ocean Racing Club man. Pronounced 'Ahh-o-ahh-see', your RORC man pads into French restaurants at the head of his crew all wisecrack, navy reefer, wet foot and wrinkled trouser. He foots the bill, eats the flowers and conducts an owlish reconstruction of the race, using bread rolls. Then you have your powerboat racers, collecting up cups like station platform buffet attendants; your converted ship's lifeboat men collecting liquid detergent containers and hoping to think up something to make with them; your canal cruising men with wives embroidered all over with anchors, and your beginners . . .

Which brings us back to where we started on the subject of the language. The yachting terminology used in conversation singles out your tyro. His goal is to pass muster as an expert, but just let him refer to his jib-sail (jib) and the curled lip and mocking eye signal his rejection. 'It' instead of 'she', 'on' instead of 'in' a yacht, 'waves' instead of 'seas' – a hundred slips betray him.

A lot of the old-time words have gone. Kevil, timonoguy, swifter, burton, vang, snottledog, slabline and jeer have vanished with the rest; but Hawe line, bustle, gel-coat, pulpit and trim-tab replace them. A good terminologist, 'two points abaft your weather bumkin lad', can wither a conversation. A man might observe, in a lull, that he has a few bad wrinkles around his nock. The silence which follows becomes unbearable. 'Ah,' you say in desperation, 'Have you, have you? Very nasty, a wrinkled nock.' You whistle tunelessly and begin reading a fire extinguisher.

It is a dangerous fact that probably thirty per cent of medical people are yachtsmen. Go to a doctor. He looks at your club tie. 'What have you got?' he asks. He means what sort of boat. He argues antifouling for half an hour until all the old women in the waiting room are clicking away impatiently, then gives you a letter to a specialist. The specialist reads it. 'Got gribble, eh?' he says. 'Breathe in slowly.' The surgeon has a gaff cutter and fancies his arm with the sail needle.

Imagine having guests for the weekend. 'You're in here, Mildred,' we say, opening the door to the cupboard under the stairs, 'Jack can have the shelf in the airing cupboard and I thought we might put Betty behind the tank in the loft.' Smiling their approval they begin struggling into their uneasy apportionments, ramming their belongings into any gap they can find, laughing as heads clank and thud against pipe and rafter. The scene is barely different from the allotment of bunks aboard a boat where sane human beings who own bedrooms with en suite bathrooms at home will clamber onto narrow plywood ledges like roosting sparrows or crawl deep into dank tunnels reeking of polystyrene and diesel oil.

The sardonic term 'accommodation plan' attached to glossy brochures of new boats shows a series of tiny compartments like a bird's egg collection, misleadingly labelled aftercabin, saloon and fore-cabin. Colour photos heighten the charms of each, showing a family of smirking dwarfs sprawling at ease or laughing hysterically over the chart table (a touch of realism here) while mother dishes up cold stew. What is not shown is the metamorphosis which takes place at sea. If you took a waiting room of NHS patients and tipped it on its ear, you'd have a fair idea.

Rheumy down below

Your new owner, treasuring the belief that his deck won't leak, enjoys a false state of bliss equal to that of the learner-driver bucketing down a pedestrian precinct in defiance of his gibbering instructor.

'It's an integral structure and deck leaks are a thing of the past,' explain salesmen chuckling at this nostalgic concept. '. . . a little localised condensation perhaps . . .'

Condensation below shroud plate bolts and the deck edge joint are still quaintly referred to as leaks and regarded by wives as the personal property of their husbands. No praise is forthcoming when these are dealt with, but a note of suppressed satisfaction is evident when they reappear.

'I suppose you know that your leak's back over the cornflakes,' they crow, implying that it has been wandering around somewhere. 'Condensation,' he snaps, pouring milk on his Puffed Rice. It sinks. Some boats drip like a shampooed sheepdog. Given an autumnal nip in the air Old Harry and his crew, snoring best bitter, can kick up more condensation than a tea urn in a tin privy.

Interior design winkles cheque-books out of pockets faster than an impressive hull shape; provided a 22 ft boat sleeps six it can look like a stuffed marrow. Below, they are little miracles of planning. So is a family mausoleum, which might go better to windward if given mast and rudder.

Yachtsmen love looking below in other people's boats. 'I can't wait to see how you're laid out,' enthuses Percy. He rattles down the ladder. There is an oaken thud and a moan. Visitors to boat shows scuttle in and out of cabin doors like a French bedroom farce, while salesmen intone their commentaries on folding table and crash-down wash-basin.

'When not in use as a chart table it hinges up to form a vanitory mirror in the optional after stateroom,' they explain. The inevitable outcome of this little innovation will whip a smile off the new owner's face like the gas bill. He comes racing below to plot a position.

'I think she's been sagging down a bit,' he says, worriedly lowering the chart table. He finds Percy's wife Doris, who has a bust like the wall of death and who buys her foundation cream from a builder's merchant, confronting him like HMS *Rodney*.

Yachtsmen used to be content with sitting headroom, emerging blinking into the sunlight from dark mahogany tunnels, half-concussed and with their jackets buttoned to their trouser flies. The less room they had the more they felt the urge to shuffle around down there. You had only to sit down with a plate on your lap and huge bums would home in like a traction engine rally. 'I wonder if I could squeeze past?' someone would inquire squeezing past. You would lift ravaged features dripping gravy. Nowadays headroom is mandatory. Salesmen nurse a smouldering hatred for those tall, thin visitors in corduroy caps who rise up damningly out of forehatches.

Yacht designers would have no problems over accommodation if only crew would go aboard stark naked, empty handed and willing to lie down flat at once; it is personal gear that causes the problems and first thing in the morning all boats look like upended puppet theatres. 'Individual locker space, while not actually generous, is in fact adequate for essentials,' write boat reviewers carefully. A Trappist monk would be pushed to find stowage for his breviary and skull. Lockers vary from vast and misleadingly generous vaults guarded by wan-faced and groaning figures recumbent on the lid to tiny tabernacles containing a dribble of brown water and a sprouting onion.

The chart table drawer is traditionally the communal back yard to be stuffed with everything from baffling navigational free gifts presented by YM to corks, dud batteries

and doll's knickers. The table itself is designed exactly an inch too short to take a folded Admiralty chart. There at bay sits our navigator surrounded by his electronic toys like nursery breakfast with Teddy, Noddy and Roland Rat. Being the only flat place in the boat when the saloon table is stowed it is in constant demand. Father raises a hand of protest as the big pan of boiled potatoes hovers. 'How am I supposed to plot our position?' he inquires peevishly, secretly wishing he knew. 'It's no good. I'll have to put a short leg in!' he declares, making for the ladder. Mother, with inspired timing, puts the pan on the bottom step.

Old Harry has no such positional difficulties. Scorning a chart table and parallel rules he works swiftly and deftly with elbow and pipestem. His computations once brought him to a theoretical harbour entrance in mid-Channel. 'I've got a fixed red, a fixed green and the leading lights dead in line ahead,' called down his novice helmsman proudly.

'The galley has received special attention,' claim brochures truthfully. There is a sink that fills on starboard tack and a tap that dribbles on port, an icebox sandwiched between hot stove and engine and, by courtesy of the designer's faulty sums, a deep and cavernous locker that would turn a potholer white with dread and down which the breadboard disappears never to be seen again. The paucity of working top area would tax a brain surgeon. The interior decor is a long stride away from horsehair and paraffin fumes. 'We decided to bring in a design expert,' say builders, as though they had dragged him in struggling and sobbing. We get a hairy deckhead and a black leather toilet seat.

The heart of a small cruiser is the toilet arrangement. Smaller boats have a chemical thunderbox defiantly lodged between the forward bunks as though it had just backed into an already overcrowded lift, and it has a plastic curtain that offers about as much real privacy as a Freemason's apron on a windy beach. Bigger boats have a proper compartment with a trick door like a magician's cabinet, and in which trying to undress is about as easy as playing the double bass in a confessional. It has a shower fitting accurately aimed at the toilet roll and a basin tucked under the sidedeck where face washing is carried out to an accompaniment of thuds and curses.

There is no way in which the more delicate functions of the morning toilet can be reconciled with the remarkable accoustics of this compartment. The ship may have been resounding with activity one moment but the second that somebody enters it falls as silent as the British Museum reading room. On either side and separated by a half inch of ply figures lie alertly, while the luckless occupant within moves with the stealth of a hunting panther. Somewhere in the crystal silence a skylark trills her thread of sound.

Perhaps, though, we must turn to Old Harry's saloon in search of that age of Edwardian elegance and the era when paid crew rode their bucking pipecots under the cascading navel pipes, spurred on by the promise of a free sack of coal at Christmas.

We descend into a dank and dripping grotto, bright with dangling bean tins, haunted by four generations of wet flannel and burnt toast, where brown linoleum curls back grinning with copper tacks awaiting the stockinged foot. It offers about as much real cheer as Knaresborough Castle dungeon. All it lacks is manacles, a salt lick and the Count of Monte Cristo rapping out messages. Maritime historians flock to study Old Harry's artefacts and a woman in a kaftan once tried to rub his brasses. There was an insurance surveyor rash enough to sneak aboard with his moisture meter. It took one sniff at that dripping ambience, then took off into the fantail like a pig after truffles.

In the immediate postwar years there were thousands of old boats to be bought for a song, a swan-song in many cases. The usual fate of boats laid up in a mud berth at the outbreak of a war which wasn't expected to last all that long was that they shifted on a big spring, fell over into their berths, filled on the next tide and became a crab's home. Gradually they settled into the mud, their exposed side bleached by sun and wind, the immersed side waterlogged but preserved. I wintered aboard one such rescued hulk and crabs continued to hatch out in her bilge so that at night they'd be scratching and rustling down there like cinema-goers unwrapping sweets. I fed them bacon rind. These boats could be odd to sail, hulls and rudders warped and distorted, good on one tack, unmanageable on the other like some Dr Jeckyll and Mr Hyde combination that called for some modifications to the Rule of the Road and a bilge pump that could have emptied the Grand Union Canal.

Built for a 'nurl

The test of a dinghy was to waggle her transom. If the stem stayed still or waggled, a second later she needed new gun'nels, breasthook, nails and knees; if it responded at once then you'd found the wrong boat.

They lay in creeks and gardens, saltings and farmyards, sheds, backyards, upside down housing hens – or on end sheltering old men who sat, spat and grumbled. Prices ranged from five bob to a fiver (upper crust stuff) and there were crab-haunted wrecks that were to be had for a shifty half-hour under cover of darkness. It was a boy's paradise because nobody had got around to wagging the finger of caution in those days.

There were nostrums of tar and cement, paint and canvas, tingles of timber or lead, tarpaper and tarpaulin.

'In glue and dust I put my trust and if that don't cure her putty must' sang the longshoremen eyeing potential buyers. Carbolic soap applied to gaping clinker seams of dried-out boats got you afloat with a foaming wake until such time as the planks took up and squeezed it out.

A boat might have more sprung butts than a beginner's day at a riding stables; she could have a hogged sheer, weeping garboards, rotted futtocks and gribble up her trunk but there'd always be a buyer, wild of eye, wearing shorts and subsisting on peanut butter who would take the job on, ripping, stripping, chipping, whipping, re-equipping and finally disappearing when the writ was nailed to her mast. In the post-war years there were big old hulks, shorn of their lead keels, at £100 a ton, floating drunkenly, high as dead dogs above the marron grasses, bought by syndicates of dreamers, busted, Tahiti-bound and learning guitar from five bob tutors.

Those were the salad days of tore-out buying. Forgotten boats long since sunk in their wartime mudberths to be dug out, emptied of mud, and indignant crabs, for the price of their gear in store. The pre-war years weren't bad either.

There was always a buyer and longshoremen knew it. 'Leaks enough ter keep her sweet,' they'd say, avoiding your eye. 'She'd row on a dewy lawn . . . why no lad, that ain't *rot*, that's water softening.' If a boat was so slack in her fastenings that she leaked and creaked like a Moses basket they'd say she was 'Givin' to it', therefore seakindly. You got to distrust any boat with a shiny pump handle.

Then there was performance. 'She was built for a 'nurl,' they'd explain, hinting at aristocratic requirements above the average . . . 'I seen that boat overtakin' Ryde ferry!' This was not unlikely, recalling the flogging progress of those lovely old paddlers. Those boats had always withstood the ultimate gale when ocean liners were going down like cinema organists and titled but craven owners were reassured by their paid skippers, who would get a sack of coal at Christmas for their stalwart behaviour.

A serious boat hunter also needed to be a drama critic. Longshoremen could express every facial emotion from affronted dignity to straight-eyed candour, from the trembling lip of pained parting to the nobility of sacrifice; it was like a treat trip to the Old Vic. Oh they wouldn't 'let her go' to just anybody (it had to be an unmitigated berk!). Oh they really ought to ''ang on to her' (correct, she'd sink if they didn't). I remember just such a man. He was called Ricky's Dad, hugely trousered, with a belted paunch, no collar, evil humoured and shrewd as a ferret. Breathing bottled ale and with a dripping baby under a vast arm, he drew a sketch of the boat on a fag packet with his free hand. 'Two quid,' he said, speaking round a dog-end and doubling the price we'd been told. 'Well I got ter live,' he explained in a cloud of smoke and ash, posing the question, 'I'm a human bean like anybody elst!' It would have saved time if we'd flushed the notes down the privvy there and then. When you turned that boat upside down and looked up at the leaks it was like being in a Planetarium. We launched her to see if she'd

take up. She did. She took up a position in 10ft of water, us having forgotten to take the ballast rocks out of her.

They had (have?) many sales lines, the most common being the 'other buyer' device. This implies a figure lurking impatiently just out of sight, cash-in-hand, but the owner anxious to be fair, for God's sake, feels honour bound to give you first refusal. You should just refuse and run for the hills. An on-the-spot offer is called for and on-the-spot is exactly where you are. I once bought a steel boat with concrete in her like that; if the boat had been in the concrete instead of the concrete in the boat she'd have been fine.

The 'Can't-bear-to-part-with-her' owner is another classic. He's only selling her to you because he likes you and believes you'll get the best out of her. This turns out to be the ballast, a teapot and two cushions. There's also Mr 'Must-sell-for-personal-reasons'. This can mean that Old Dobbin has been auctioned off, the Squire has foreclosed, Little Nell has done it proper this time and the well has run dry; or it can mean that he bought a ragbag and wants to hand it on – fast.

You got to see the insides of a variety of homes, from conservatories with water colours and cane furniture, to the steaming rain forests of drying nappies in back kitchens, through which you fought like a Chindit evading an ambush towards the backyard shed where the gear was stored. Magnetos though were traditionally stored in the airing cupboard along with monumental bras like a breeches-buoy and a tin box containing an enema.

Pocket and birthday money dictated the spending of us lads, which left us fewer options than a man on a flagpole, but we did once aim above the target. Sixteen feet of varnished mahogany, sails, everything, two years old and ten quid at Sunbeam Yard in Cowes. In Scout uniform, to imply integrity, hair smarmed, we approached the yard manager, speaking in the fluting tones we imagined to be indicative of a refined upbringing and families of substance. He bit it. He spent half an hour showing us boat and gear. 'Tell you what we'll do,' fluted David,

111

the financial wizard of our partnership, 'we can offer two bikes, an airgun and a tent, also, *also* a weekly payment of nine pence.'

He drew a long and shuddering breath, appearing to consider this offer. 'And *I'll* tell *you* what *I'll* do,' he said, speaking like a watch-your-weight machine. We waited expectantly, prepared to consider any reasonable modification to our offer. 'I'll count up to *ten*,' he bellowed suddenly, '. . . and if you young buggers haven't gone you'll get my boot up your asses!'

The immediate post-war years brought the Director of Small Craft Disposals (DSCD) bonanza. Buyers were invited to put in their tenders. The boats lay in huddles. Harbour launches, landing craft, MTBs and Air Sea Rescue boats, assault boats, jolly boats, sinking boats and boats never intended to sink, like a certain HDML.

Alec, doyen of the waterfront layabouts, my prototype Old Harry and a man whom I have actually *seen* standing in his nightshirt in front of the kitchen fire on a Sunday morning, playing an accordion while his wife was at church with the Children Of Mary, had his own notions about putting in tenders. He made a derisory offer, drilled a small hole in the HDML while looking her over and repeated his offer, a nicely calculated month later, when she was by then so low in the water that no more offers of any sort were forthcoming. His offer was accepted at speed by a grateful Director of SCD. Alec cut a snottledog to fit the hole and paid his ten quid. The only other expenditure was a backhander to a mate in the Fire Service who had access to a portable motor pump.

I am sure there must be cases of true love and romance flowering against a backdrop of sheet winch and kicking strop, where even the impregnability of the oilskin suit (which renders even the basic call of nature a feat of amazing contortion) fails to insulate wearers from the hot flush of passion and its denouement, but not in my experience. Boats and sexual fervour go together like nuns and skateboards and the best you can hope to achieve is a 'laughing fellow rover' relationship. At 3 A.M. on a wet night off the Nab mirth is not unrestrained.

I once lent my boat to a honeymoon couple. What I had forgotten is that of the four available berths aboard two were a bare five feet long and the other two were encased for half their length in a sort of plywood tunnel. Now, I'm as broadminded as the next man, I've read the Kama Sutra *and my imagination is well developed, also I have faith in the ingenuity of the desperate but . . . . After a week (they had borrowed the boat for a fortnight) they returned looking strained and remote. They booked in at the first hotel they came to.*

Come back to me my love

That I was very much younger at the time goes without saying. No man – no yachtsman anyway – in his prime, with all his marbles and skilled in the ways of small cruisers, could have laid his skinny neck upon the block so willingly.

My intentions were utterly base from the outset.

There was this girl (we'll call her Polly in wary deference to the laws of libel) and there was this cruiser available to me on very special terms for a weekend charter. 'How about a little cruise, just you and me?' I asked, mastering the tremor in my voice and trying to stop my eyebrows from slashing up and down like a typewriter ribbon. I explained that it would be a gentle cruise for two, teaching her to sail, panoramic views of St Albans, wind-in-her-hair, etc.

She not only fell for it but she also fell for my hint that if mum and dad knew they'd only worry about us being a bit short-handed – after all there were perils of the deep to consider. Yes, indeed there were, I thought laughing evilly. We fixed a date and I set about my preparations with the naivety of a country lad buying a wristwatch down in Liverpool Street Station loo. We would arrive in Poole Harbour at about 1930 on Saturday evening and I would anchor round the back of Brownsea Island in perfect solitude. First there'd be drinks in the cockpit and redshanks calling, sunset painting the placid canvas of dimpling water while supper cooked below. Then the candlelight, the wine, eyes meeting shyly across the tiny table then . . . then . . . God, I could scarcely bear to think of it.

I still can't, but for totally different reasons. With the bitter hindsight of nearly forty years on, I can now see that my plans were about as conducive to harmony as a trombonist in a telephone kiosk. The mockers were on them. The gods of fate were rolling around with mirth clutching their aching ribs. The steamy and passionate picture I envisaged was about as appropriate to the occasion as a clockwork bow tie at a Civic Dinner. The cruiser was a converted chicken shed powered by a gaff mainsail like a roadman's tent and an engine with stalactites hanging from the exhaust and a backfire like a lifeboat maroon. It had once shot a duck. The decor below decks would have made a Mexican confessional look like a Regency ballroom. The saloon mattresses were horsehair and so genuine that I could have fed them bran mash. It had a double bunk.

Polly's nose wrinkled slightly upon being shown over this little Argosy and she peered into the forecabin like a novice potholer looking down Kettle Bottom, but she accepted my assurances that the buckled pipecot and dribbling cork fenders were evidence of sturdy seagoing durability. In due course we set sail. That, in itself, evokes a bitter laugh because the peak halyard parted immediately and the jib, which was too long in the luff, set like a Roman toga in classical folds and scallops.

We had the tide fair through Hurst on the last of the ebb, the sun shone, the cliffs fell astern and we left the Needles as we lifted to the brief popple to seaward. I glanced covertly at my watch and saw that we were bang on schedule for Poole and passion. Then the sun disappeared. Half an hour later it began to drizzle and ten minutes after that the breeze fell to a flat, wet calm. 'We'll start the engine,' I said, uttering that historic sentence which has been the catalyst of a thousand nautical nightmares.

But need I go on . . . need I mention that it refused every ingenuity until, hours later, it banged suddenly into life only to settle down to a spluttering jogtrot that gave us bare steerage way? We arrived many hours later off Poole not, as planned, in the soft flush of evening on the young flood, but at damn near midnight in a profound blackness and the ebb just starting. In panic I had breached the gin and tonic, made up wholesome doorsteps of bread and turkey paste and pointed out the Pole Star. Polly,

115

muffled in every outer garment I possessed, sat mute and threatening on the companionway step showing as much animation as a train-spotter on a wet Sunday in Pontyprid. It wasn't too late though, I kidded myself. We'd soon be anchored; then why not the cosy lamplight, slim hands holding man-sized cocoa mug, eyes looking up at me with little-girl rapture? Why not? I'll tell you bloody why not.

With the engine giving two knots, shaking like a Cuban band and stinking like a wet sheepdog and with the tide now ebbing at one and a half knots, few brows will need to be furrowed in the effort of working out our progress. It took over an hour to get past the chain ferry and to reach a likely spot (the nearest) for anchoring, and by then I was desperate. The wine alone had cost five shillings! Polly had that awful aura of menace about her that only women can achieve; a looming glower, unspeaking but the message plain as neon. Then I saw the mooring buoy. So did the engine and uncannily, like a three-legged lame dog spotting a cat, it took off on all four pots.

In those days it was not so long since the flying boats had left their base at Poole, and their huge circular mooring buoys, like great rubber-tyred wheels, were still dotted around. They had a ringbolt dead in the centre and to attach a line you had to *jump on to them with a rope's end* . . . I couldn't ask Polly to do that, now could I? Nowadays I could, mate.

Shall we just pause here to reflect upon this option? Nowadays I'd no sooner push my luck to that extent than I'd wear a shoulder-bag in a lumber camp. Consider the odds. Black night, sluicing ebb, clattering engine and a woman with her jaw set like an Easter Island statue – a buoy upon which I proposed to leap. If you programmed a computer with that lot it would come up with a print-out on the *Titanic*. Despite having youth on my side I was no athlete; a basket of oranges and a low-cut singlet didn't make me Nell Gwynne. Give old Ned the shepherd treacle toffee a minute before the sheepdog trials and you couldn't louse up an operation better.

Desperate situations call for desperate measures. 'Right then, Polly,' I piped, 'What I'm going to do is this . . .' I went on to explain the simple workings of gear and throttle. She grunted. At this point readers may frown and nod impatiently as if faced with some whodunnit plot of utter and infantile banality in which the butler plods wearily and predictably to an anticlimactic *dénouement*. I was also showing off. I positioned the boat downtide and inched ahead until the huge and swirling buoy was close to port. Then, rope in hand, I poised myself and jumped.

I landed squarely. 'Hold her steady,' I encouraged. The engine was bellowing. Did she really think that 'steady' sounded like 'ahead'? Polly banged the throttle wide, slipping the leash on all twelve horses, my yells were drowned, I was transfixed and the rope slid through my nerveless grasp as the boat went surging by. I watched that fat-ass transom (the yacht) disappear into the night while I crouched on that lurching buoy like a peeled shrimp on some nightmare canapé, howling instructions and prayers learned at my mother's knee.

For some minutes I watched the sternlight grow fainter, then it vanished to be replaced by a green – then circling slowly and at some distance to a red and green. Good girl, I thought warmly, she's using some initiative. She might also have used a harpoon with an explosive warhead or an iron ball on a chain but with less effect. She was handling that throttle like pumping a Blake. I now know what a charging rhino looks like through the popping saucer eyes of the transfixed hunter. Luckily she only struck the buoy a glancing blow, causing it to rotate – a maritime merry-go-round upon which I squatted, cursing shrilly. Was it the second time round or the third when I leapt? Anyway, leap I did, wrapping my arms around the shrouds, legs dragging through the water.

'Why, you stupid *cow!*' I howled, dragging myself aboard. No after-dinner speaker anxiously groping around for his notes under the table has gingered a Presidential wife to greater heights of outraged wrath than did that unwise outburst. I spent the rest of that night in the mil-dewed misery of the forecabin with the anchor rattling and the deck dripping like Mother Shipton's wishing well. At 0400 the pipecot collapsed. At 0800 I rowed her ashore in awful silence to put her on a train.